Inflation!   Money, Jobs and Politicians

Inflation!

Money, Jobs, and Politicians

Raburn M. Williams
University of Hawaii

with a foreword by
Gary M. Walton

AHM Publishing Corporation
Arlington Heights, Illinois 60004

PRINTED IN THE UNITED STATES OF AMERICA
7129

Contents

Foreword

The Atmosphere of Crisis

An economic and political crisis of growing proportions is being witnessed today in the U.S. and in other areas of the world. As shown in the polls, many Americans are expressing discontent and a lack of confidence in many major American institutions. A dramatic illustration of voter outrage over high taxation and perceived government waste was the landslide passage of Proposition 13 in California in 1978. Subsequently, numerous pieces of legislation, limiting the growth of state government expenditures and/or taxes, have passed in other states. Most startling of all has been the call for a constitutional convention to require the federal government to balance its budget. At this time, out of the 34 required, 31 states have called for such a constitutional convention.

The current crisis is manifesting itself in many other ways as well. For instance, the soaring cost of hospitalization and medical treatment is also viewed as a crisis, and government representatives are proposing legislation to deal with it. The crisis in housing, especially rental units, is mounting daily. Legislation proposing rent controls has been approved in both Berkeley and Santa Monica, California. In response, apartment owners there, and those in other areas anticipating the possibility of rent controls, are converting their rental units into condominiums. Of course, this decreases the supply of available rentals, pushes rents higher, and encourages more political clamor for rent controls. The sector crisis currently receiving the greatest attention is that of energy, where shortages are pervasive and prices are sharply moving upwards. Finally, there is the supermarket, where the homemaker and daily shopper helplessly view the upward march of prices. The underlying cause of each of these "sector crises" has a common source, namely inflation. They also have a common cure. Few studies match *Inflation: Money, Jobs, and Politicians,* by Raburn M. Williams, for clarity of exposition about the true causes of inflation and why the needed steps to correct the current plight have not been taken.

No Government Constraint

One striking consequence of the horrible years of the Great Depression was a fundamental change in public attitudes about social ills and the role of government in the life of its citizens. Prior to 1930, the general public and government representatives widely believed that government should be limited and that the best government was that which governed least. President Cleveland maintained that while the people should support the government, the government should not support the people. President Wilson stated that the history of liberalism was the history of restraints on government power. As the Depression deepened, such attitudes began to change, and a clamor for government "to do something" arose in its place. The first steps taken were to protect the remnants of the economic institutions and businesses still operational in the early 1930s. Promoted by a government committed to general assistance, vested interest groups of all types increasingly sought and received government aid. Small businesses received the Robinson-Patman Act; large corporations gained protection by way of higher tariffs; unions were given the right to strike for the first time; banks and other financial institutions received protection by way of the Federal Deposit Insurance Corporation; social security helped those in retirement and nearing retirement; and the agricultural sector obtained price supports. These and other measures have expanded over time culminating in the years of Johnson's Great Society and the decade of the 1970s. Today, the degree to which citizens rely on government is greater by far than anything the early New Dealers could have imagined possible. As new social ills arise, the first inclination is to turn to government to seek solutions.

In keeping with the times, liberal court rulings on the interstate and the general welfare clauses of the Constitution permitted the federal government to engage in activities and to initiate programs that would have been considered unconstitutional by many people (and the courts) a half century ago. More recently, this lack of a constitutional constraint has been accompanied by an absence of a budget constraint, and as a result, government has grown enormously.

Because the federal government faces no effective budget constraint, existing programs can be expanded and new programs begun without serious regard for funding or cost. In addition, since each bill is considered separately, Congress does not vote on legislation with the total legislative package in mind. Special interest groups and administration bureaucracies, either potential or existing, lobby for expansion and support on each specific bill. Legislators receive most of their information about bills from those groups standing to gain from the legislation and who lobby vigorously and effectively. Alternatively, the unwary taxpayer, who will pay for the costs, often does not find it worthwhile, either individually or collectively, to lobby or bring information to bear against each individual piece of legislation. As a result, persistent pressure is exerted on government to expand existing programs and to add new ones.

The growth of government spending, unchecked either by constitutional and/or budget constraints, has consistently exceeded corresponding increases in taxes, and the federal budget records a string of deficits that now number 19 out of the last 20 years. The persistence of these deficits, and the methods by which they have been financed, have propelled the present inflation, which is fueling the current crisis. Adding to the crisis is the feeling that government cannot be trusted and that it is increasingly less responsive to the people and instead more and more responsive to special interest groups and entrenched government bureaucracies.

Inflation: Characteristics and Causes

The price level now stands at more than five times that of 1933, or four times that of 1929. Today the purchasing power of the dollar is only one fourth of what it was 50 years ago. The following table, which illustrates the consumer price index (CPI) for all items over the last 10 or 11 years shows that the value of the dollar has fallen approximately in half.

The subcategories of the table show that the average price of food and beverages has slightly more than doubled in the last decade and that of housing has just about doubled. Apparel and upkeep has less than doubled, rising about 60 percent; transportation costs have increased about 85 percent;[1] medical care has gone up by 120 percent, and entertainment has risen by approximately 75 percent. Although there are differences in price movements in these categories, the increase in prices is quite general. The inflationary problem is not specific to any one category or industry. It is a general phenomenon.

Despite proclamations by government officials, there is no real mystery about inflation. The incurrence of inflation, like the incurrence of pregnancy, is dependent upon many factors. Yet, it has but one cause. Inflation is not caused by oil sheiks, labor unions, corporate monopolists, or other alleged conspirators. Although an increase in monopoly power may permit changes in relative prices, the overall price

---

[1]Of course, more current information on gasoline prices would change this figure upward.

Consumer Price Index for Urban Wage Earners and Clerical Workers, Annual Averages and Changes, 1967-78 (1967 = 100)

Year	All Items	Food and Beverages	Housing	Apparel and Upkeep	Transportation	Medical Care	Entertainment	Other Goods and Services
	Index % Change	Index % Change	Index % Change	Index % Change	Index % Change	Index % Change	Index % Change	Index % Change
1967	100.0 —	100.0 —	100.0 —	100.0 —	100.0 —	100.0 —	100.0 —	100.0 —
1968	104.2 4.2	103.5 3.5	104.0 4.0	105.4 5.4	103.2 3.2	106.1 6.1	105.7 5.7	105.2 5.2
1969	109.8 5.4	108.8 5.0	110.4 6.2	111.5 5.6	107.2 3.9	113.4 6.9	111.0 5.0	110.4 4.9
1970	116.3 5.9	114.7 5.4	118.2 7.1	116.1 4.1	112.7 5.1	120.8 6.3	116.7 5.1	116.8 5.8
1971	121.3 4.3	118.3 3.1	123.4 4.4	119.8 3.2	118.6 5.2	128.4 6.5	122.9 5.3	122.4 4.8
1972	125.3 3.3	123.2 4.1	128.1 3.8	122.3 2.1	119.9 1.1	132.5 3.2	125.5 2.9	127.5 4.2
1973	133.1 6.2	139.5 13.2	133.7 4.4	126.8 3.7	123.8 3.3	137.7 3.9	130.0 2.8	132.5 3.9
1974	147.7 11.0	158.7 13.8	148.8 11.3	136.2 7.4	137.7 11.2	150.5 9.3	139.8 7.5	142.0 7.2
1975	161.2 9.1	172.1 8.4	164.5 10.6	142.3 4.5	150.6 9.4	166.6 12.0	152.2 8.9	153.9 8.4
1976	170.5 6.8	177.4 3.1	174.6 6.1	147.6 3.7	165.5 9.9	181.7 9.5	159.8 5.0	162.7 5.7
1977	181.5 6.5	188.0 6.0	186.5 6.8	154.2 4.5	177.2 7.1	202.4 9.6	167.7 4.9	172.2 5.8
1978	195.3 7.6	206.2 9.7	202.6 8.6	159.5 3.4	185.8 4.9	219.4 8.4	176.2 5.1	183.2 6.4

Source: Bureau of Labor Statistics.

level cannot be increased in a sustained fashion. Economic aberrations may cause temporary price bulges, but inflation over several years can only be caused by the growth of the money supply relative to the growth of production of goods and services.

Economists have a historical record of the causes of inflation that goes back not just a decade or so, but one that covers more than 4,000 years. Evidence is available on inflation and its causes stemming from ancient Egypt, ancient Athens, and ancient Rome, when governments sometimes debased the coinage by lessening the precious metal content per coin minted and thereby expanding the money supply. There is detailed information available on the "great price revolution" in 16th-century Europe, caused by the influx of New World treasure. Sound data on the causes of every inflation in American history begin with those in colonial times and continue through to the present.[2] These data include the fall in the value of

[2]See Anna J. Schwartz, "Secular Price Change in Historical Perspective." Universities-National Bureau Committee for Economic Research, Conference on Secular Inflation. Supplement to *Journal of Money, Credit and Banking* Vol. 1, Pt. 2 (February 1973): 243–69.

the "continental" in the American Revolution, the fall in the value of the greenback in the Civil War, and the fall in the value of the dollar in World War II.

Every inflation in the history of mankind has been preceded by a growth in the money supply relative to the growth of the goods and services produced. Furthermore, no inflation has ever been brought under control except by a constraint on the growth of the money supply relative to the growth of the goods and services produced.

West Germany's and Switzerland's experience with inflation early in the 70s offers enlightening instruction for our purposes and shows clearly that our inflation is of our own making. West Germany and Switzerland were far more vulnerable to the real shocks produced by OPEC (Organization of Petroleum Exporting Countries) and the failure of agricultural crops than was the U.S. They still managed, by a determined reduction of their monetary growth (below the excessive rates reached in 1972), to lower their inflations to the vanishing point.

Similar monetary constraint was not undertaken in the United States, and the rate of monetary expansion (relative to goods) has accelerated. In the 1960s, output in the United States increased at an average of 6.6 percent per year. The quantity of money increased by an average of 10.6 percent, or 4.0 percent per year faster than output. Inflation also grew an average of 4.0 percent per year. Between 1970 and 1978, output increases averaged 2.1 percent per year, with the rate of growth in the money supply averaging 9.5 percent per year. This 7.4 percent difference in the rate of expansion in the money supply relative to output matched exactly the 7.4 percent inflation rate of that period.[3]

Recent excessive monetary growth stems largely from the willingness of the Federal Reserve to accommodate the Treasury in its sale of bonds to pay for the persistent deficits created by Congress. Since the Federal Reserve authorities are not free of political influence, it is unlikely that appropriate monetary restraint can be developed until the persistent government deficits are first eliminated. To repeat, the only effective means of reducing inflation is to restrain the growth of the money supply. There is little hope that this can be accomplished until the deficits of the federal government are eliminated for it is primarily the Federal Reserve's purchase of bonds issued by the Treasury to pay for these deficits that is causing the expansion of the money supply relative to the goods and services.

---

[3]See the chart "Inflation Results When Money Increases Faster Than Output" by David I. Meiselman in *Forty Centuries of Wage and Price controls: How Not to Fight Inflation,* ed. Robert Schuettinger and Eamonn Butler (Washington, D.C: The Heritage Foundation, 1979).

Inflation and Government Deceit

Despite these historical facts, the Carter administration and earlier administrations as well have turned to wage and price controls to attack the inflation problem. Politically, such controls serve a vital purpose for they shift the blame for inflation from government mismanagement to the private sector. This is most unfortunate for a variety of reasons, but perhaps worst of all, it encourages our leaders to lie about what they are doing and why they are doing it. For instance, as prices soared by 1.1 percent in April 1979, the government's response was that it was largely up to the purchasing public to stop the spiral. Alfred Kahn, the administration's chief inflation fighter, told reporters, "The government can do some things but not a helluva lot; for the most part it rests with the consumer." Charles Schultze, chairman of President Carter's Council of Economic Advisors, said he expects the administration program to take hold later in the year, moderating inflation generally, and in particular, the rate of increase for food.[4] In short, for political reasons, key government officials have repeatedly lied to the American public about the causes of inflation, and such deception is not merely to avoid responsibility. In periods of inflation, debtors gain at the expense of creditors, and government is our largest debtor. Inflation also allows more spending and public sector expansion without explicit legislation of new or additional taxes; as the taxpayers are pushed into higher tax brackets, public sector imperialism becomes automatic.

Because of such misinformation, a majority of Americans, by accounts from the polls, are willing to accept wage and price controls. They want action, and at least controls indicate a willingness on the part of government to do something. And yet, as past experience has shown, if controls are imposed, it is soon found that the cure is worse than the disease, that inflation will not subside, and that shortages will appear and conditions will deteriorate.

The Futility of Wage and Price Controls

As with evidence on the causes of inflation, economists have extensive accounts of the effects of wage and price controls that reach back more than 4,000 years.[5] Although their disruptive effects have been displayed time and again, we can find no instance in which they ever worked effectively to curb inflation. Our experience with wage and price controls during the Nixon years is a good case in point. As shown in the following figure, Nixon's controls were imposed in August 1971, when the inflation rate was 4.5 percent. The precontrol rate of inflation was 6 percent in early 1970 and was actually falling at the time controls were imposed. The rate of

[4]Washington (UPI), May 26, 1979.
[5]Schuettinger and Butler, *Forty Centuries of Wage and Price Controls.*

Annual Rate of Inflation

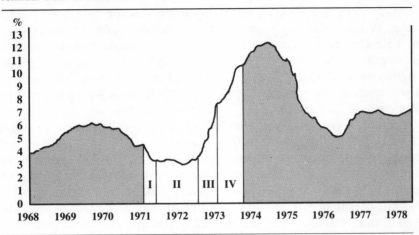

Source: U.S. Dept. of Commerce Statistical Abstract, 1978, p. 483.

inflation continued to drift down and remained around 3 percent throughout 1972, started to rise in 1973, and by the time the controls were completely lifted in early 1974 the rate was 10 percent and rising.

Rather than curb inflation, price controls actually contribute to the problem. For example, to circumvent the Nixon controls, the lumber industry regularly exported lumber from the United States to Canada, then reimported it for sale at higher, more profitable prices. Although poultry feed was not subject to controls, chickens were, and as feed became more expensive, it ultimately became unprofitable and uneconomic to feed chickens. As a result, millions of baby chickens were slaughtered instead of taken to market, and shortages of chicken became pervasive. As it became more profitable to sell fertilizers and chemical pesticides abroad rather than at home, agricultural production suffered for want of these essential inputs. These and many other similar disruptions to production made the growth rate of goods and services relative to the money supply less and therefore the inflationary situation worse than it would have been without controls.

Why Controls Fail

Wage and price controls never work because they attack symptoms rather than causes. An appropriate analogy to consider would be a teapot of boiling water. One way to stop the steam from coming out of the spout is to plug the spout. An alternative is to turn down the heat. Attempting controls is exactly like this.

Plugging the spout, alone, will never work and may lead to an explosion. Controls can be made to appear effective only if appropriate monetary constraint accompanies them. Without such a constraint, changing market conditions create economic chaos. Yale Brozen has likened a policy of price controls without monetary restraint to putting ice on a thermometer. He states, "We can put a piece of ice on a thermometer so that it will show 75 instead of 85 degrees, but the people in the room will continue to perspire in discomfort as long as we continue to pump heat into the room."[6]

Of course, it is correctly argued that prices are set by people making decisions, and in that sense, all prices are administered prices. But prices are not determined arbitrarily by human values of fairness or greed. People in business, and others negotiating contracts, determine prices according to market conditions, and market conditions today are constantly changing as a result of the expansion of the money supply. The prevalence of monopoly, or human greed, or error of judgment has not changed dramatically, nor has the ineffectiveness of controls. The one fundamental condition that has changed in the last decade and a half has been the advance in the supply of money relative to the goods and services produced.

Inflation and Social Decay

Perhaps the worst evil of price controls is that they postpone the day of reckoning, and as people's expectations adjust to the inflation, it becomes more difficult to reduce. Moreover, as inflation and dislocations continue, public confidence deteriorates. John Maynard Keynes eloquently expressed these forces in his book, *Economic Consequences of Peace:*

> Lenin is said to have declared that the best way to destroy the Capitalist System was to debauch the currency. By a continuing process of inflation, governments can confiscate, secretly and unobserved, an important part of the wealth of their citizens. By this method they not only confiscate, but they confiscate *arbitrarily;* and, while the process impoverishes many, it actually enriches some. The sight of this arbitrary rearrangement of riches strikes not only at security, but at confidence in the equity of the existing distribution of wealth. Those to whom the system brings windfalls, beyond their deserts and even beyond their expectations or desires, become "profiteers," who are the object of the hatred of the bourgeoisie, whom the inflation has impoverished, not less than of the proletariat. As the inflation proceeds and the real value of the currency fluctuates wildly from month to month, all permanent relations between debtors and creditors, which form the ultimate foundation of capitalism,

---

[6]Yale Brozen, "Inflation and Price Controls," in C. Carl Wiegand, ed., *The Menace of Inflation* (Old Greenwich, Conn.: Devin-Adair Co.), p. 151.

become so utterly disordered as to be almost meaningless; and the process of wealth-getting degenerates into a gamble and a lottery.

  Lenin was certainly right. There is no subtler, no surer means of overturning the existing basis of society than to debauch the currency. The process engages all the hidden forces of economic law on the side of destruction, and does it in a manner which not one man in a million is able to diagnose.[7]

As our current atmosphere of crisis continues to heighten, the need to implement effective measures becomes increasingly critical. The alternatives are few but clear; federal spending cannot be brought under control and deficits eliminated simply by voting new people into office. New representatives are also vulnerable to pressures from special interests.

  What is needed to offset the bias propelling growing government expenditures is a federal budget constraint firmly imposed by constitutional amendment. Of course, it raises efficiency to transfer power from the people to the representatives who then allocate resources among competing programs. But this should be done within a fixed budget constraint and not as is currently done. The present system sets no limit on the growth of government. Until one is set, the pocketbook of the American taxpayer and the well-being of the American consumer will come under continued attack.

  Our constitution promises us that no person shall be deprived of life, liberty or property without due process of law . . . nor shall private property be taken for public use without just compensation. The inflation of the last 15 years makes a mockery of our Constitution. It is an inflation we can ill afford and a mockery we should not tolerate.

  Appropriate steps to stem inflation will probably not be taken until there is much better understanding by key decision-makers and the general public on the causes of inflation and the mechanisms of controlling the money supply. *Inflation: Money, Jobs, and Politicians* offers much hope in this regard. This short, precise book is topnotch for the classroom and should be mandatory reading for all of our government representatives. I am convinced that if this were so, Congress would swiftly set its house in order and the current atmosphere of crisis would fade into history.

      Gary M. Walton
      Dean, School of Business
      University of Miami

---

[7]John Maynard Keynes, *Economic Consequences of Peace* (New York: Harcourt, Brace and Howe, 1920), pp. 235–36.)

Preface

We are now in the longest and most virulent inflation the United States has ever experienced. This short book provides a nonmathematical analysis of the causes and the effects of the current inflationary malaise. Although the approach is basically "monetarist," it also includes a discussion of many nonmonetary factors which have had an impact on the price level. Throughout this book, the analysis emphasizes the political constraints which have created a governmental bias in favor of inflation and which currently prevent the U.S. from returning to an era of price stability.

The first three chapters summarize the basic concepts of macroeconomics found in introductory textbooks. Chapter 1 is a summary of the basic concepts of public finance. Inflation, which is a "tax on money balances," is shown to be one of several methods for financing government expenditures. This explains why governments have often turned to the printing press when political constraints have limited the ability to raise revenue through the tax system. Moreover, the indirect effects of inflation on the progressive income tax structure and the inflationary transfer of wealth from the owners of government bonds to taxpayers in general provide additional financial motivations for the government to inflate.

Chapter 2 develops the relationship between monetary growth and the rate of inflation within the context of the circular flow of income and expenditures. The Federal Reserve's role in controlling the money supply is analyzed within the context of the government's budget constraint. This approach to the determination of the money supply clarifies the relationship between budget deficits and money creation which is so important in chapter 1.

Chapter 3 discusses the infamous trade-off between inflation and unemployment and explains why the trade-off exists in the short run, but not in the long run. It also explains why the dynamics of the "accelerationist Phillips curve" has produced a "political business cycle."

These macroeconomic concepts are then used to analyze economic policymaking and its consequences from the Johnson administration to the Carter administration. Chapter 4 explains how the current inflation originated with Johnson's failure to raise taxes to finance the war in Vietnam. Chapter 5 discusses how that inflation wreaked the international monetary system and forced the United States, Western Europe, and Japan to adopt floating exchange rates. Nixon's efforts to reduce the rate of inflation in 1969 which precipitated the 1970 recession are described in chapter 6. Chapter 7 discusses the political attractiveness but the economic folly of Nixon's wage and price controls. In Chapter 8, Nixon's game plan for the 1972 election is analyzed within the context of the political business cycle. Chapter 9 analyzes the macroeconomic effects of the worldwide crop failures and the Arab oil embargo of 1973–74. Chapter 10 shows why Carter's economic policies brought on the dollar crisis of 1978.

Chapters 11–13 discuss several policy issues of current importance. Chapter 11 explains the serious distortions inflation has created in our tax system and discusses some current proposals for tax reform. The macroeconomic effects of recent increases in the minimum wage and the social security payroll tax are analyzed in chapter 12. Chapter 13 looks at the likely effects of deregulating the airlines and the trucking industry.

The last chapter looks ahead to the 1980 election. Carter's anti-inflation program is examined in the context of the political business cycle. The chapter also includes a critique of Carter's wage and price guideline program and an analysis of the macroeconomic impact of the rise in oil prices following the revolution in Iran.

Finally, I would like to acknowledge my debt to several individuals who have provided invaluable assistance to me. Professor Roger Leroy Miller (University of Miami) is primarily responsible for my writing this book. Without his encouragement and help, the book would probably not have been finished. I am also fortunate to have received detailed comments on earlier drafts from professors Thomas Havrilesky (Duke University) and Carl Dahlman (University of Wisconsin). Bill Reisner was extremely helpful in editing the final draft, and Roger Williams, the AHM editor, provided me with unfailing support and assistance.

Illustrations

The fortress-like Federal Reserve Bank,
Maiden Lane and Nassau Streets, New
York City.   (Wide World Photos)

1
Inflation and Government Revenue

The year 1979 marks the 25th anniversary of continuous price increases in the United States. In 1954, the consumer price index (CPI) declined about one half of a percentage point. Prices have increased every year since then. Goods and services which sold for $10 in 1954 cost about $27 in mid-1979. The current inflation, one of the longest in U.S. history, has survived mandatory wage and price controls, voluntary guidelines, and four recessions. What is even worse is that the long-run secular rate of inflation has been accelerating. Consumer prices rose at an average rate of 1.7 percent per year during 1955–65. But since 1966, the rate of inflation has accelerated to an average of over 6 percent per year. The purpose of this book is to explain the causes and the effects of this postwar inflation.

Inflation is almost always created by government. Government creates inflation by printing money, and that expansion in the money supply enables the government to finance some of its expenditures. This is the most obvious reason why government creates inflation. Historically, inflation has usually been associated with governments lacking the political will or power to collect enough taxes to pay for government expenditures. Unable to finance their expenditures through taxation, these politically weak governments resorted to printing money to pay their bills. John Maynard Keynes explained *inflationary finance* in the following way:

> A government can live for a long time, even the German government or the Russian government, by printing money. Let us suppose that there are in circulation nine million currency notes, and that they have altogether a value equivalent to 36 million gold dollars. Suppose that the government prints a further three million notes, so that the amount of currency is now 12 million; then, in accordance with the above

theory, the 12 million notes are still only equivalent to 36 million dollars. In the first state of affairs each note equals four dollars, and in the second state of affairs each note equals three dollars. Consequently, the nine million notes originally held by the public are now worth 27 million dollars instead of 36 million dollars, and the three million notes newly issued by the government are worth nine million dollars. Thus by the process of printing the additional notes the government has transferred from the public to itself an amount of resources equal to nine million dollars just as successfully as if it had raised this sum in taxation.[1]

The German Weimar Republic is an extreme example of a weak government which survived for some time through inflationary finance. On April 27, 1921, the German government was presented with a staggering bill for reparations payments to the Allies of 132 billion gold marks. This sum was far greater than what the Weimar Republic could reasonably expect to raise in taxes. Faced with huge budget deficits, the Weimar government simply ran the printing press to meet its bills.

During 1922, the German price level went up 5,470 percent. In 1923, the situation worsened; the German price level rose 1,300,000,000,000 times. By October of 1923, the postage on the lightest letter sent from Germany to the United States was 200,000 marks. Butter cost 1.5 million marks per pound, meat 2 million marks, a loaf of bread 200,000 marks, and an egg 60,000 marks. Prices increased so rapidly that waiters changed the prices on the menu several times during the course of a lunch. Sometimes customers had to pay double the price listed on the menu when they ordered.

Of course, such astronomical rates of inflation wiped out any debts denominated in marks. Investors in fixed income financial securities lost everything. Debtors, however, gained immensely. The heaviest losses were suffered by the middle class and pensioners. In the end, inflation produced social divisions which completely destroyed Germany's democratic institutions. The massive transfer of wealth from creditors to debtors destroyed the savings of the middle class and played no small role in the subsequent rise of Hitler and the National Socialist Movement.

Meanwhile, in Russia, the Bolsheviks were financing their civil war by printing rubles. In 1920, 90 percent of government revenue to finance the costs of government and the military expenditures associated with the civil war was obtained by printing money. By 1922, the ruble was worth only 1/200,000 of its prewar value. Moreover, the redistribution of wealth from creditors to debtors was welcomed by many Communists as a way of expropriating the remaining monetary wealth of the bourgeoisie. The printing press was described by the Russian minister of finance as "the machine gun of the proletariat, mowing down the monied classes."

[1] John Maynard Keynes, *A Tract on Monetary Reform* (London: Macmillan, 1923), pp. 37–39.

Governments can also finance their budget deficits by borrowing instead of printing money. This method of financing budget deficits is far less inflationary because the sale of bonds to the public reduces private purchasing power. Purchasing power is merely transferred from the public to the government, leaving the total amount essentially unchanged. *Debt finance,* however, can only postpone the plight of a fiscally irresponsible government. A government that finds it politically unacceptable to limit its expenditures to available tax revenues today will find it just as difficult to use future tax revenue to pay interest to those who hold government bonds. Sooner or later, the bondholders and the government will realize that debt finance simply postpones the real tax burden resulting from government expenditures. When the fiscal responsibilities of government are not honestly faced, the government eventually has to resort to printing money to finance the deficit.

Inflation does indirectly what taxes do directly. For this reason, economists sometimes refer to inflation as a "tax on money balances."

An important economic principle lies behind the practical choice of methods used to finance government expenditures. If the government is to succeed in purchasing an additional quantity of national production, private purchases of available output must be reduced. Taxing, for example, directly reduces the funds available for private expenditures on national output. Government borrowing from the public also absorbs funds that the private sector could otherwise have used to purchase goods and services. This is because the purchasers of government bonds could have used those funds to purchase goods and services themselves, or they could have loaned the funds to someone else who would have spent them.

Printing money, on the other hand, does not directly reduce the private funds available for purchasing output as does taxation or borrowing. Instead, printing money causes inflation which indirectly reduces the output purchased by the private sector. As prices rise, each individual's initial money balances will purchase fewer goods and services. When individuals are faced with a reduction in the purchasing power of their money balances, they typically desire to replace at least part of the depreciation by using some of their income to increase the number of dollars they are holding. This diversion of income to build up the number of dollars in each individual's money balances reduces the funds available for spending on goods and services, allowing the government to acquire more of the available output of goods and services. Inflation does indirectly what taxes do directly. For this reason, economists sometimes refer to inflation as a "tax on money balances."

Of course, printing money, like all taxes, creates economic distortions in the allocation of resources. All taxes tend to reduce the supply of the commodity or service being taxed. The income tax, for example, distorts the choice between labor and leisure. When earned income is taxed, the relative cost of not working falls. Consequently, workers tend to take longer vacations and retire at an earlier age. The same sort of effect occurs when printing money is used to provide government revenue. Since inflation is a "tax on money balances," it reduces the real quantity of money people desire to hold. In order to maintain a given amount of purchasing power in the form of money balances, individuals must use some of their spendable income to add to the dollar value of their money balances in order to offset the depreciation of the purchasing power of each dollar. Inflation, then, represents the cost of maintaining purchasing power in the form of money balances. If individuals expect future inflation, they will economize on the amount of money they hold.

This tendency of the public to economize on money balances limits the extent to which printing money can finance government expenditures. The real resources that can be obtained by the government by printing money are the rate of inflation times the desired purchasing power that individuals want to hold in the form of money balances. As the inflation rate rises, the tax on each dollar of money balances increases. Each dollar is depreciating at a faster rate. However, this will induce individuals to hold less purchasing power in the form of money balances. At some point, higher inflation rates actually yield fewer resources to the government because the reduction in the demand for real money balances outweighs the increase in the inflationary tax on each dollar.

Uncle Sam [is] the largest beneficiary of the inflationary transfer of wealth from creditors to debtors.

Periods of *hyperinflation,* when prices go up by more than 50 percent per month, are characterized by a widespread "flight from money." In the German inflation of 1921–22, for example, government revenue from printing money was high at the beginning. But once the people learned to anticipate future inflation, they began to cut down on the purchasing power held in money balances. Workers were paid several times a day and were given time off from work so that they could spend their money immediately. If they held money for even a short period of time, their cash would become valueless. Thus, individuals had an enormous incentive to buy goods the minute they received their money. The German government couldn't print money as fast as people could bid up prices, so the real value of the total money stock actually shrank dramatically. This "flight from money," of course, reduces the real resources yielded to the government by printing even more money. By 1923, the Weimar government received fewer and fewer resources from printing money even though they were doubling the money supply every week.

Not only does an expansion in the money supply directly finance some of the government's deficit, the resulting inflation also produces indirect benefits for the government. A rise in the price level reduces the real burden of the government's debt. The U.S. government's outstanding debt to the public, for example, was over $500 billion by 1979, making Uncle Sam the largest beneficiary of the inflationary transfer of wealth from creditors to debtors. Inflation allows the government to make payments to creditors with dollars that are worth less than the dollars the bondholders initially loaned to the government. Since the cost of servicing the government debt is a future tax liability to the public, unanticipated inflation tends to transfer wealth from the holders of government bonds to the taxpaying public in general.

At the same time that inflation reduces the real burden of the government debt, it also increases the yield from the tax system without the need for any new tax laws. This results from the progressive rate structure of the United States income tax. Tax collections go up substantially as prices rise because inflation pushes more and more people into higher and higher tax brackets, even though the real purchasing power of their before-tax income remains the same. The effective income tax rate increases resulting from inflation are greatest for those in the low and middle income groups.

The chart on page 6 shows (1) the income tax as a percentage of income for various income groups and (2) the tax rate for individuals with the same real income after doubling the price level.

Still another advantage inflation brings to the United States government— one which sounds highly technical but which can be important to a company's profits—involves inventory profits and depreciation. Until recently, the most common method of accounting for inventories was the first-in, first-out (FIFO) method. Under the FIFO method of inventory accounting, the costs of production used in calculating profits on sales out of inventories are based on the costs of producing the oldest units in the inventory. Because historical costs rather than inventory replacement costs are used in calculating profits, the apparent income of a corporation using this method of accounting would be artificially inflated by the "paper profits" on its inventories produced by inflation. Paper profits on the sale of inventories produced in the past are not available for capital investment or distribution as dividends. These funds must be earmarked for use in replacing those inventories at the new, higher price. Since corporations must pay taxes on those illusory inventory profits, many corporations have recently switched to a last-in, first-out (LIFO) basis of accounting because of inflation. This method uses the cost of producing the last units added to the inventory in calculating the profit on sales out of inventories. This cost will usually be much closer to the actual cost of replacing depleted inven-

Income Tax as a Percentage of Income Before and After Doubling the Price Level

Income tax as a percentage of income (Family of 4 with standard deductions, 1978 tax rates)		Income tax as a percentage of income for the same before-tax real income but after doubling prices	
Real Gross Income	% Tax	Nominal Gross Income	% Tax
$ 5,000	0%	$ 10,000	4.4%
10,000	4.4	20,000	12.6
25,000	15.4	50,000	27.6
50,000	27.6	100,000*	41.3
100,000*	41.3	200,000*	53.3
1,000,000*	66.6	2,000,000*	68.3

*Tax rates of unearned income. Income from the sale of personal services is subject to a 50 percent maximum rate.

tories during periods of inflation, avoiding most but not all of the tax on the "paper profits" shown on inventories.

Moreover, the depreciation allowances which corporations can deduct from their taxable income are based upon the original cost of capital equipment. Corporations pay taxes on net profits—the difference between all revenues and all allowable expenses. Depreciation allowances are allowable expenses under the tax law to compensate for all the depreciation, or wear and tear, on buildings and equipment. With inflation, the real value of depreciation allowances is reduced. This means the allowances are not adequate to replace buildings and equipment at the inflated prices which will prevail when the need for replacement comes. The reduced real value of these depreciation allowances, then, amounts to an increased tax on the return on capital.

Even though democratic governments may choose to finance some of their expenditures through money creation, honesty would require that inflationary finance take place within the context of an indexed personal and corporate income tax rate structure and indexed government bonds. Under an indexed tax, tax brackets, personal exemptions, and depreciation allowances would be replaced by a number multiplied by a price index. With this indexation, a cost-of-living increase in an individual's money income, which is solely due to inflation, would not push him or her into a higher tax bracket. Similarly, the base for calculating capital gains and inventory profits would be adjusted to eliminate paper profits arising from general inflation. To eliminate the transfer of wealth from bondholders to the government resulting from inflation, the government would be forced to borrow only with purchasing power bonds. For example, bonds would be issued with an interest coupon of, say, 3 percent. On each interest date, the par value of the bond would be adjusted to take account of the inflation, or deflation, which had taken place since the bond was issued. If the rate of inflation was 10 percent during the first year, then the par value of the bond would be adjusted upward from $1,000 to $1,100. The interest paid that year would then be 3 percent of $1,100 or $33. At maturity, the accumulated change in the purchasing power of the dollar would determine the final settlement. If the price level had tripled, then the bondholder would be paid $3,000.

The use of inflation to indirectly raise tax rates and reduce the real burden of the government debt is basically fraudulent and incompatible with democratic control of government. Unfortunately, politicians have a natural preference for spending taxpayers' money—to win the support of those who receive the benefits —and an equally powerful incentive to avoid voting for explicit tax increases. For this reason, the most important single act to contain long-run inflation may well be to index the tax system and federal debt in order to reduce the contribution that inflation makes to government revenue.[2]

[2]See Milton Friedman, *Tax Limitation, Inflation and the Role of Government* (Dallas: The Fisher Institute, 1978).

John Maynard Keynes (1883-1946) at 56 years. (Historical Pictures Service, Inc., Chicago)

2
Monetary and
Fiscal Policy

The branch of economics which deals with the study of inflation and unemployment is called *macroeconomics.* The circular flow of income and expenditures, one of the central concepts of macroeconomics, provides an especially convenient framework for analyzing the causes of inflation and unemployment.

The basic idea behind the circular flow of income and expenditures is really quite simple. When goods and services are sold, the receipts from the sales become the income of individuals in the economy. A business firm's sales revenue becomes the wages, salaries, rent, interest, and profits earned by individuals who supplied the services and raw materials used in reducing the firm's output. These payments to individuals are the sources of income used, in turn, to purchase the goods and services produced by other business firms in the economy. Since all sales revenue becomes someone's income, production can always generate an equivalent amount of income.

This identity between *gross national product* (GNP), which is the total value of all the goods and services produced, and *national income,* which is the total of all wages, salaries, interest, rent, and profits received by individuals, was first recognized by the 19th-century economist Jean-Baptiste Say. Unfortunately, Say mistakenly jumped to the conclusion that there could never be an imbalance between aggregate demand and aggregate supply because "supply creates its own demand." Say failed to realize that this is the case only if individuals in the aggregate desire to spend on goods and services an amount which is exactly equal to total national income. If individuals in the aggregate desire to spend more than the total national income on goods and services, expenditures on output will exceed the value of goods and services currently being produced and inflation is inevitable.

Although spending on goods and services in excess of current production can be temporarily satisfied by reducing inventories, sooner or later business firms will raise their prices and increase production in response to this excess spending. On the other hand, if desired expenditures fall short of total national income, business firms will be unable to find enough buyers to purchase the current output, so prices will tend to fall and production will decline.

When total expenditures on goods and services are exactly equal to total national income, the economy is said to be in *flow equilibrium*. Economists use the term *flow* to designate a process that occurs continuously through time. For this reason, flows are measured in units per time period. Total spending on goods and services, national income, and gross national product are all flows and thus are measured in terms of dollars per year. Economists make a crucial distinction between flows and stocks. A *stock* is an accumulated quantity of something existing at a particular moment in time. The physical quantity of goods held in inventories, for example, is a stock. When the flow of total spending on goods and services is exactly equal to the flow of gross national product, the physical stock of inventories will neither rise nor fall.

The main cause of *flow disequilibrium* between expenditures and production lies in imbalances between the supply of money created by the Federal Reserve System and the desire of the public to hold that stock of money. The money supply is made up of all the currency in circulation plus deposits at commercial banks. Because the money supply is a stock, it is measured in terms of dollars, not dollars per year. Economists basically use two different operational definitions of the money supply. The narrow definition of the money supply, called M_1, consists of currency in circulation plus checking accounts at commercial banks (also known as demand deposits). A more broadly defined quantity, called M_2, is equal to M_1 plus most savings accounts (time deposits) at commercial banks. People have a certain desired stock of money that they want to have on hand as a general source of purchasing power. Moreover, the stock of money individuals and businesses desire to hold has been closely related to total national income. Since the early 1960s, for example, individuals and businesses have desired to hold a stock of M_2 money balances equal to about 40 percent of national income. If the Federal Reserve creates either "too much" or "too little" money, the stock disequilibrium between the demand for money and the supply of money quickly leads to a flow disequilibrium between expenditures on goods and services and current production.

Each individual can adjust his or her money balance to any level desired by spending more or less than received. If a man desires to hold more money than he currently has on hand, he can increase his current money balance by spending less than he receives. If his current money balance is greater than the amount he desires to hold, he can reduce his money balance by spending more than he received. Consequently, when the public finds itself with a larger stock of money than it collectively desires to hold, each individual will attempt to spend it or loan it to someone else who will spend it. In the modern vernacular, money in excess of the desired amount "burns a hole in your pocket." The problem that arises when there is an excess supply of money is that the public as a whole cannot get rid of those unwanted money balances. When everyone rushes out to spend unwanted money, it just ends up in the pockets of others who are just as intent on getting rid of it. As a result, efforts to reduce money balances start to resemble a game of musical chairs, with unwanted dollars always in motion looking for a place to settle. Collectively, the public cannot reduce the supply of money since one individual's expenditure has to be another individual's receipt.

Although doomed to failure, the attempt to reduce money balances creates a flow disequilibrium between production and expenditures on goods and services. In terms of the circular flow of income and expenditures, desired expenditures on goods and services will exceed national income as individuals attempt to spend more than they receive. Initially, this imbalance between total production and total spending will just cause inventories to drop, but sooner or later businesses will respond to this excess demand for goods and services by raising prices.

When everyone rushes out to spend unwanted money, it just ends up in the pockets of others who are just as intent on getting rid of it.

Fortunately, this increase in prices tends to return the economy to equilibrium. Individuals and businesses usually desire to hold money balances equal to a fairly stable fraction of total income. Since the increased income associated with the sale of output at higher prices will increase the demand for money, the excess supply of money will tend to be eliminated. Prices will eventually stabilize at the level which makes the demand for money equal to the supply of money. Collectively, individuals cannot reduce their money balances, but their attempts to do so will raise prices (and increase income) until the demand for money is equal to the supply of money. At that equilibrium price level, individuals in the aggregate are willing to hold the stock of money created by the Federal Reserve System and, consequently, will desire to spend on output an amount exactly equal to their income, keeping the circular flow of income and expenditures in balance.

The public currently wishes to hold M_2 money balances equal to about 42 percent of national income. This fraction has been essentially constant for over 20 years. The fact that the ratio of M_2 to nominal income has been constant implies that the M_2 money supply and nominal income grow at the same rate. Since nominal income is equal to real output times the price level, this relationship also implies that prices should rise at the same rate as M_2 money balances per unit of output. This can be readily seen in the following chart which plots the gross national product price deflator and the ratio of M_2 to total output (real gross national product).

The ratio of the M_1 money supply to nominal income has been falling at the rate of about 2.7 percent per year. This implies that nominal income increases about 2.7 percentage points faster each year than the annual rate of increase in M_1. Although M_2 has increased at a faster rate than M_1 during the postwar period, changes in their rates of growth have been very similar.[1]

Although the chart shows that there is an extremely stable relationship be-

The Consumer Price Index and the Ratio of M2 to Total Output

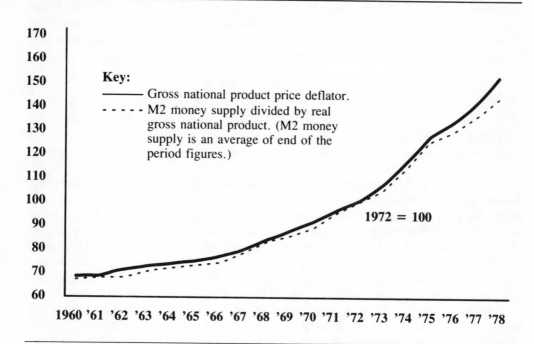

Key:
——— Gross national product price deflator.
- - - - M2 money supply divided by real gross national product. (M2 money supply is an average of end of the period figures.)

1972 = 100

Source: Data collected from *Federal Reserve Bulletin,* Federal Reserve Bank of St. Louis.

[1]For an excellent discussion of this relationship between the money supply and Gross National Product see David Meiselman, "Worldwide Inflation: A Monetarist View," in *The Phenomenon of Worldwide Inflation,* ed. David Meiselman and Arthur Laffer (Washington, D.C.: American Enterprise Institute, 1975).

tween the price level and M_2 money balances per unit of output, it does not necessarily imply that there is a close relationship between the M_2 money supply and prices. A 10 percent increase in the M_2 money supply could cause prices to rise by 10 percent with production remaining constant, or it could cause output to increase by 10 percent leaving prices unchanged. Both of these events would be consistent with the relationship indicated by the chart. As a rule, changes in the rate of growth in the money supply do have significant short-term effects on output (real gross national product). In the long run, there is a close relationship between the rate of monetary growth and the rate of inflation, but this relationship is often obscured by the long lags involved.

If the rate of monetary growth accelerates, so does aggregate spending on goods and services. At first, this increase in spending merely causes inventories to fall, but about six months later, businesses react by increasing employment and production. At this point, there will be very little effect on prices because labor and raw material prices tend to be fixed by price contracts. However, the increased demand for labor and raw materials associated with the business expansion will eventually bid up wage rates and raw material prices. These increased costs of doing business will be passed on to consumers as higher prices. The time lag between an acceleration in the rate of monetary growth and an acceleration in the rate of inflation is about two years. Once it gets started, inflation develops a momentum of its own as expectations of future inflation are embodied in wage contracts.

Similarly, when the rate of monetary growth suddenly slows down, prices may continue to rise at their former rate for some time because of a continuing increase in labor and raw materials costs. These inflationary cost pressures cannot last for long, however. As costs rise in the face of a slowdown in the rate of total spending, businesses lay off workers and reduce production. As excess capacity and unemployment rates rise, unemployed workers will be willing to accept lower wage rates in order to get jobs, and excess capacity will eventually cause the prices of raw materials to drop. A reduction in the rate of monetary growth will produce a drop in the rate of inflation about two years later, but a temporary rise in unemployment is usually one of the costs of reducing inflation once it has generated a momentum of its own.

Control of the money supply is clearly at the heart of economic policies aimed at controlling the growth of total spending. The money supply is essentially determined by the Federal Reserve System's Board of Governors and Open Market Committee (collectively known as the Fed). The Federal Reserve System was created by an act of Congress in 1913 to fill the role in the United States that central banks fill in European countries. It is headed by the Board of Governors whose seven members are appointed by the president, along with the advice and consent of the Senate, to terms of 14 years. The Fed's monetary policy is, by design, substantially independent of both Congress and the president. The 14-year terms of the seven governors, one of which expires every two years, makes it impossible for any president to create a majority on the board within one four-year term. Federal Reserve operating expenses are paid out of the interest earned on the government bonds it holds. This interest amounted to $8.455 billion in 1978. (However, the Federal Reserve lost approximately $633 million in its open market and foreign exchange operations, leaving only $7.822 billion.) The Fed's current expenses for running the Federal Reserve Banks and the Board of Governors amounted to $706 million. After paying $63 million in dividends to member banks and adding $47 million to its surplus account, the rest of its interest earnings were given back to the U.S. Treasury! As a result of its earnings, the Fed is one of the only government institutions which is not subject to congressional discipline through the "power of the purse" since its expenditures are not subject to the appropriations process.

Once it gets started, inflation develops a momentum of its own as expectations of future inflation are embodied in wage contracts.

Once each month, the Federal Open Market Committee gathers at 9 A.M. in the marble boardroom of the Board of Governors on Constitution Avenue to draft guidelines as to how rapidly the money supply should grow in the month ahead. The Open Market Committee is made up of the 7 board members and the 12 presidents of the regional Federal Reserve Banks (only 5 of whom have voting rights at any one time). This committee issues directives concerning the purchase or sale of government securities (called open market operations). When the Fed buys government bonds from the public, it pays with a check drawn on itself, which immediately injects that amount of new money into the economy. When it sells bonds, it takes money out of circulation as the purchaser draws on a checking account to pay for the bond. These directives of the Open Market Committee are carried out by the trading desk in the fortresslike Federal Reserve Bank of New York in the Wall Street financial district.

When the Federal Reserve injects new money into the economy by buying a bond, the seller of the bond usually deposits the check in a checking account at a commercial bank. The commercial bank can then earn interest on that deposit by loaning the funds to businesses and consumers or by purchasing financial securities. When these funds flow out of the commercial bank, the money supply in the hands of the nonbanking public goes up again. Moreover, most of these new money balances will eventually be deposited in checking accounts, creating still further increases in the money supply.

The commercial banks are required by law, however, to hold some of their deposits back from investments or loans. These are held in the form of *bank reserves,* which consist of vault cash and deposits at Federal Reserve Banks. The Federal Reserve directly controls the reserve deposit ratio through its power to set the reserve requirements imposed on its member banks. These reserve requirements limit the possible expansion of the money supply. If all the newly created money was deposited in checking accounts, each new dollar injected into the economy by the Federal Reserve could potentially increase the money supply by the inverse of the reserve requirement. For example, if the reserve-deposit ratio were 20 percent, each new dollar injected into the economy by the Federal Reserve would produce a $5 increase in the money supply.

This potential expansion would occur only if all newly created money were redeposited at commercial banks, so as to produce a return flow of reserves to the banking system. In reality, some of the newly created money will be held as currency. This prevents a complete return of reserves to the commercial banking system and acts as a drain on reserves. Since some portion of newly created money is held in the form of currency, the *actual* expansion of the money supply is considerably less than the inverse of reserve requirements. With today's reserve requirements and propensity to hold currency, every new dollar injected into the economy through open market operations increases the M_1 money supply (currency plus demand deposits) by about $2.50.

Still another tool available to the Fed in implementing its monetary policy is its power to make loans to commercial banks. These loans are called *advances* and *discounts.* An officer of a member bank desiring a loan can simply place a telephone call to the discount window of a Federal Reserve Bank and request an advance (loan) using U.S. government bonds as collateral for the loan. Such loans by the Fed have the same effect on the money supply as open market purchases of bonds; they inject new money into the economy, causing a multiple expansion of the money supply.

The Federal Reserve does not use its *advances* and *discounts* as a major instrument of monetary policy, however, because it does not have as direct control over these loans as it does over its open market operations. The Fed cannot initiate the loans made through the "discount window"; it can only grant or refuse a loan request by a commercial bank. The interest charged on advances and discounts is, however, controlled by the Federal Reserve. This is the famous *discount rate* that gets so much attention in newspaper articles about the economy. By raising the discount rate above the prevailing market interest rate, the Fed discourages commercial banks from borrowing because banks will have an incentive to borrow only if they can lend the borrowed funds at a higher rate of interest than they have to pay the Fed. Access to the Fed's discount window is also limited directly, aside from the effect of the discount rate.

While the Federal Reserve is busily making monetary policy, Congress and the president are making decisions regarding the level of government spending and taxation, or *fiscal policy.*

It is a widely held belief that *deficit spending*—government spending in excess of tax revenue—adds to total spending on goods and services and thus puts upward pressure on the price level. Indeed, many individuals attribute inflation almost solely to deficit spending. However, the actual relationship between deficit spending and inflation is even more complex than it may seem. Increases in government spending and tax cuts have the immediate effect of increasing the budget deficit, which requires additional borrowing by the Treasury. The degree to which deficit spending increases total expenditures on output depends principally on the Fed's response to the government's increased borrowing.

If the Fed chooses, it can buy Treasury bonds in open market operations to "make room" for the new Treasury borrowing. This will inject new money into the economy and produce a multiple expansion of the money supply. Economists call this option *monetizing the government debt.* Since an increase in the ratio of money to output causes higher prices, this method of financing the deficit will be inflationary. However, the Fed can force the Treasury to borrow in the private capital market by refusing to monetize the debt. If it chooses this alternative, private citizens must purchase the newly issued Treasury bonds with income that could have been spent on goods and services. Thus government borrowing from the private sector directly reduces the income available for private expenditures. Therefore, the potential purchasing power added to the economy through a tax cut or an increase in government spending is offset by the government borrowing necessary to finance the resulting deficit.

There is another indirect channel through which a fiscal stimulus can affect spending even when the money supply does not actually expand. John Maynard Keynes, the British economist who has had such a profound effect on modern economic thinking, pointed out that interest rates are the cost of holding money, because cash and checking account balances do not earn interest.[2] When interest rates rise, it becomes more costly to hold money balances rather than interest yielding financial securities. Consequently, to the extent that deficit finance adds to the competition for borrowed funds and thus increases the rate of interest, individuals have an incentive to invest some of their money balances in order to take advantage of the higher interest rates. These loans made from previously idle money balances prevent the government deficit from completely "crowding out" private expenditures, leaving some net fiscal stimulus. However, most economists would agree that this effect is fairly minor.

The popular belief that deficit spending is inflationary results from the histori-

[2]John Maynard Keynes, *The General Theory of Employment, Interest, and Money* (London: Macmillan, 1936).

cal correlation between big budget deficits and rapid increases in the money supply. Traditionally, the Federal Reserve has been very concerned about the general level of interest rates. Since increases in the government deficit tend to raise interest rates and lower the price of government bonds, the Federal Reserve has usually "leaned against" the fall in the price of government bonds by becoming a purchaser of government bonds, thus monetizing the government debt. Economists sometimes refer to the practice of monetizing the debt during periods of heavy Treasury borrowing as an *even keel policy.* There have been a few notable exceptions to this standard practice, however. Whenever the Federal Reserve has forced the Treasury to borrow in private capital markets, the inflationary effects of government deficits have been minor, although the negative effect on real growth resulting from the crowding out of private investment remains significant.

William Nordhaus, Yale University
economics professor who served on
President Carter's Council of Economic
Advisers, photographed in January, 1977,
in New Haven, Connecticut. (Wide World
Photos)

3
The Trade-Off Between
Inflation and Unemployment

Inflation produces many economic distortions when markets cannot or do not adjust to the changing purchasing power of the dollar. The lagged adjustment of wages to changing price levels, for example, is one of the principal causes of fluctuations in the unemployment rate. Decisions regarding employment depend critically on the relationship between wage rates and the price of the final product. The incentive to expand output and increase employment is directly related to the impact of such expansion on profits. When an employer hires additional workers, the increase in profit is equal to the price of output times the additional production minus the cost of hiring the extra labor. For example, if the price at which output is sold is 50¢ and an extra worker will add eight units of production per hour to total output, the manufacturer can profitably employ an extra worker only at wage rates less than $4.

In his *General Theory of Employment, Interest, and Money,* John Maynard Keynes argued that money (or nominal) wages were relatively rigid, at least in the short run, and were determined by outside (exogenous) institutional factors, not supply and demand. Keynes' General Theory deals essentially with the theoretical implications of that assumption of wage rigidity.[1] Because of this assumption, an increase in the rate of total spending would tend to raise selling prices, but nominal wage rates would remain unchanged or rise less rapidly than prices. When the prices of finished goods increase and wage rates do not, employers have an incentive to increase employment and output. Keynes argued that the unemployment rate

[1]John Maynard Keynes, *The General Theory of Employment, Interest, and Money* (London: Macmillan, 1936).

could be reduced by expansionary monetary and fiscal policies, because he assumed that wage rates would rise less rapidly than the prices of final products, thus enhancing the profitability of greater production and employment.

The assumption of relatively rigid money wage rates is a central feature of most economic theories which relate employment to changes in total spending. If wages are sticky in an upward direction, expansionary monetary policies tend to increase employment and production. Similarly, it follows that if wage rates are sticky in the downward direction, monetary policies which reduce total spending would increase unemployment rates because wage rates would tend to rise relative to prices.

What has become increasingly apparent in recent years is that the stimulative effect of expansionary monetary policies on employment depends critically upon the speed at which people change their expectations of inflation. Inflation affects employment levels because workers are deceived and cannot accurately predict the real purchasing power their wages will have in the months ahead. If the rate of inflation were always anticipated with complete accuracy, the real purchasing power of wage rates would be unaffected by changes in the rate of inflation. In such a world of perfect foresight, any change that occurred in the rate of monetary growth would not affect real output and employment. All that would change would be the rate of inflation.

In reality, changes in the inflation rate have significant effects on output and employment. Because it takes some time to become aware that the underlying rate of inflation has changed, long-term labor contracts and other relatively rigid institutional arrangements are slow to adjust.

Inflation affects employment levels because workers are deceived and cannot accurately predict the real purchasing power their wages will have in the months ahead.

Even when the rate of expansion of the money supply is reduced, individuals continue for some time to base their expectations on the earlier inflationary experience. Workers continue to demand higher wages in an effort to protect the purchasing power of their wages from the high rates of inflation which both the workers and their employers expect will persist. Often, these inflationary expectations are frozen into two- or three-year contracts. As a result, wages tend to rise relative to the actual prices of final products when the rate of monetary growth is reduced, increasing unemployment. A pay increase of 10 percent a year for three years, negotiated when prices were rising at a comparable rate, can then become an impossible burden if the rate of price inflation is cut in half.

When the rate of monetary growth accelerates, the opposite effect occurs. Workers fail to demand full compensation for a higher rate of inflation, because it is largely unanticipated. Wage rates fall relative to the prices of final products, and employment increases. Although it is true that unanticipated inflation makes it easier to get and keep a job for a while, this is only because money wages lag considerably behind the rising cost of living, causing real wages to fall.

The trade-off between inflation and unemployment was the subject of much discussion in the late 1950s and early 1960s. The British economist, A. W. Phillips, established an empirical relation linking one value to the other.[2] This has become known as the *Phillips curve.* The curve showed that price stability had a calculable cost in unemployment, and a low level of unemployment had a similar cost in inflation. The influence on policymaking of this seemingly inescapable relationship was set forth in a discussion by Paul Samuelson and Robert Solow of the Massachusetts Institute of Technology at the American Economic Association meeting in 1960:

> #1 In order to have wages increase at no more than the 2½ percent per annum characteristic of our productivity growth, the American economy would seem, on the basis of twentieth century and postwar experience, to have to undergo something like 5 or 6 percent of the civilian labor force's being unemployed. That much unemployed would appear to be the cost of price stability in the years immediately ahead.
>
> #2 In order to achieve the nonperfectionist's goal of high enough output to give us no more than 3 percent unemployment, the price index might have to rise by as much as 4 or 5 percent per year. That much price rise would seem to be the necessary cost of high employment and production in the years immediately ahead.[3]

However, what fixed relationship economists thought they had detected began to become unglued as the decade of the 1960s neared its end. It became clear that ever higher rates of inflation were required to keep employment high. A comment from economists Mary Hamilton and Albert Rees expressed the growing doubts about the Phillips curve concept:

> We regard the construction of a plausible Phillips curve from annual data for a long period of time as a *tour de force* somewhat comparable to writing the Lord's Prayer on the head of a pin, rather than as a guide to policy . . . the authors of Phillips

[2]A. W. Phillips, "The Relationship between Unemployment and the Rate of Change of Money Wage Rates in the United Kingdom, 1861–1957," *Economica,* Vol. 25 (November, 1958), pp. 238–99.
[3]Paul Anthony Samuelson and Robert M. Solow, "Analytical Aspects of Anti-Inflation Policy," *American Economic Review* (May, 1960).

curves would do well to label them conspicuously "Unstable—Apply with Extreme Care."[4]

An explanation for the diminishing usefulness of the relationship Phillips had discovered was advanced by several economists in the late 1960s, particularly the University of Chicago's Nobel Laureate, Milton Friedman.[5] Their analysis stressed the importance of inflationary expectations mentioned earlier. If workers can correctly forecast current and future prices, there should be no relationship between the ratio of wages to prices and the rate of inflation. An across-the-board increase in wages and prices which leaves the ratio of wages to prices unchanged will not alter anyone's decision to hire or fire workers. When everyone's expectations about current and future prices are correct, unemployment should come to rest at a "natural rate" of about 5.5 to 6 percent. Fluctuations in the unemployment rate around this "natural rate" occur only because expectations about current and future prices are incorrect.

The precise relationship between unemployment and inflation depends on how individuals form their expectations. Postwar analysis of the relationship between inflation and unemployment can be divided into two stages. The first stage was the inverse relationship between inflation and unemployment represented by the Phillips curve. The stability of this relationship depends on how rigidly people hold their expectations of future inflation. If everyone thinks that prices will rise at 2 percent per year, any inflation rate above that level will be underestimated, and this will push the unemployment rate below its "normal level." Conversely, any rate of inflation below 2 percent per year would push the unemployment rate above its "normal level." So long as the expected rate of inflation remains rigidly at 2 percent per year, there will appear to be a stable trade-off between inflation and unemployment.

During the 1950s and the early 1960s, a forecast of 2 percent inflation would not have been bad for most years. In some years, the inflation was higher, and in others, lower, but these fluctuations were to a large degree random and fairly small. Starting in the mid-1960s, however, a rigid expectation of 2 percent inflation would have led to very large forecasting errors. The *average* rate of inflation for the 1966–78 period was over 6 percent per year. Moreover, the deviations from the average rate of inflation had a much different pattern from that which prevailed earlier. Instead of deviating from the average in a random way, inflation rates in the 1966–78 period have become highly correlated. If one year's rate of inflation

[4]A. R. Rees and M. T. Hamilton, "The Wage-Price-Productivity Perplex," *Journal of Political Economy,* Vol. 75 (February, 1967).

[5]Milton Friedman, "The Role of Monetary Policy," *American Economic Review,* Vol. 58 (March, 1968). Also see Milton Friedman, Nobel lecture, "Inflation and Unemployment," *Journal of Political Economy,* Vol. 85 (June, 1977).

was over 6 percent, the following year's rate of inflation will probably be over 6 percent, too. When inflation rates are correlated, past rates of inflation contain a lot of information about future inflation rates. As a result of this change in the pattern of inflation rates, the public's adherence to rigidly held expectations of inflation was no longer rational, and they started using a weighted average of past rates of inflation to forecast future inflation.

This shift in the way individuals form expectations caused a new relationship between inflation and unemployment. Once individuals use past rates of inflation to form their forecasts of future inflation, there is no long-run trade-off between inflation and unemployment. An increase in the rate of inflation could not permanently reduce the unemployment rate because individuals would revise their forecasts of inflation upwards on the basis of past inflationary experience. As expectations of inflation adjust to reality, the unemployment rate would rise back to its normal level. In order to maintain an unemployment rate below the "normal level," the actual rate of inflation must exceed the expected rate of inflation. But, since expectations eventually adjust upward because of past experience, an accelerating rate of inflation is required to maintain the gap between actual and expected inflation. For this reason, the new relation between inflation and unemployment is known as the "accelerationist Phillips curve."

. . . politicians are usually more concerned with the short-run consequences of economic policies than with their long-run effects. The typical time horizon for political decision-making is no further ahead than the next election.

In the practical world of applied economics, theories that clash with the wishes of policy-makers can be, and often are, disregarded. The arguments against the Phillips curve by the accelerationists have not caused it to be thrown out by economic policy-makers. In the short run, it is still possible to buy less unemployment by paying the price of more inflation. And, as we shall see in later chapters, politicians are usually more concerned with the short-run consequences of economic policies than with their long-run effects. The typical time horizon for political decisionmaking is no further ahead than the next election. For this reason, politicians are rarely concerned with the long-run consequences of their economic policies. As Keynes noted, "In the long run, we are all dead." However, the long run is approaching more quickly now as the public becomes more familiar with changing monetary and fiscal policies and learns to anticipate changes in the rate of inflation. The short-run tactics favored by politicians already are less effective than in the past and may not work at all in the future.

Nevertheless, many economic analysts have become convinced that politicians have consciously manipulated the economy in order to produce low rates of inflation and unemployment in years of presidential elections. Politicians know that high rates of inflation and unemployment are politically disastrous for incumbent administrations. Because of these political considerations, some economists, notably William Nordhaus, an economic theorist from Yale University and who served on President Carter's Council of Economic Advisors, have hypothesized that there is a four-year "political business cycle."[6]

This tendency for incumbent presidents to engineer a reduction in inflation and unemployment rates in presidential election years is clearly confirmed for the 1947–76 time period. In only six of those years did inflation and unemployment rates simultaneously decline. Four of those six occasions were presidential election years. Inflation and unemployment rates simultaneously declined 50 percent of the time during presidential election years, but only 9 percent of the time during other years.

The engineering of a simultaneous drop in inflation and unemployment is possible because of the long lag between changes in the rate of monetary growth and changes in the rate of inflation. The short-run effects of changes in the rate of monetary growth are primarily on output rather than on prices. If the rate of monetary growth accelerates, for example, so does aggregate spending on goods and services. But at first this acceleration in the rate of spending has very little effect on the rate of inflation. Businesses initially react to the increased spending by increasing employment and production. This is the favorable aspect of monetary expansion. However, the increased demand for labor and raw materials associated with business expansion will eventually bid up wage rates and raw material prices, and these increased costs of doing business will be passed on to consumers in higher prices. At this point, inflation starts to develop a momentum of its own as expectations of future inflation are embodied in wage contracts. Because of these lags, an acceleration in the rate of monetary growth will produce an acceleration in the rate of inflation about two years later.

Conversely, businesses, whose short-term costs are determined by prior contracts, initially react to a reduction in the rate of monetary growth by reducing employment and production. This is the adverse short-term effect of a restrictive monetary policy. The favorable effect of reducing the rate of inflation occurs about two years after the initial deceleration in the rate of monetary growth.

The existence of these lags may permit an incumbent administration to time

[6]William D. Nordhaus, "The Political Business Cycle," *Review of Economic Studies,* Vol. 42 (1975).

its monetary policies so that the short-term effects of monetary expansion and the long-term effects of monetary restraint simultaneously occur on election day. The incumbent president should pursue a restrictive monetary policy two or three years before the election and then switch to an expansionary monetary policy about 18 months before the election. The full inflationary consequences of the expansionary monetary policy would then be postponed until after the election.

The hypothesis of a politically motivated business cycle assumes that the Federal Reserve will cooperate with the incumbent administration's fiscal stimulus by expanding the money supply. The fact that monetary policy is controlled by the Federal Reserve rather than by Congress or the president admittedly weakens this political interpretation of the business cycle somewhat. The governors of the Federal Reserve are insulated from immediate political pressures by their 14-year terms. The Fed's independence has, in fact, caused several bitter disagreements between incumbent administrations and the Federal Reserve over the conduct of monetary policy. But the president does have persuasive powers which he can bring to bear on the members of the Federal Reserve Board. Congress and the president can also put indirect pressure on the Fed by creating the problem of financing large budget deficits.

This manipulation of the unemployment rate through expansionary demand policies raises some serious ethical questions in a democracy. Expansionary demand policies lower the unemployment rate precisely because individuals are tricked into underestimating the rate of inflation, causing them to work for lower real wage rates than they would otherwise accept. Gordon Tullock of Virginia Polytechnic Institute makes the following comment on this point:

> This whole discussion of deception as a government policy raises most interesting political problems. . . . The voters cannot adopt a policy of deceiving the workers because they are largely the same people. [The argument in favor of using inflationary demand policies to reduce the unemployment rate] must be addressed to some group which is thought of as politically powerful and capable of carrying on a policy of deceiving the workers without telling the voter-workers what it is. It is only on this elitist interpretation that it makes any sense at all. Open discussion of the desirability of fooling the worker must be based on a quite unjustified contempt for his intelligence.[7]

The growing sophistication of the electorate may be changing the old political rule that low unemployment rates on election day are always good for votes. As

---

[7]Gordon Tullock, "Can You Fool All of the People All of the Time," *Journal of Money, Credit and Banking,* Vol. 4 (May, 1972), pp. 426–30.

economist Robert J. Gordon points out, the political business cycle hypothesis depends upon the assumption that voters cannot perceive the long-run consequences of expansionary demand policies.[8] Nevertheless, voters are learning to anticipate the long-term consequences of monetary and fiscal policies, and as they learn more, they will become less impressed with unsustainable booms on election day.

[8]Robert J. Gordon, "The Demand for and Supply of Inflation," *Journal of Law and Economics,* Vol. 18 (1975).

President Lyndon Baines Johnson and
William McChesney Martin, Chairman of
the Federal Reserve Board of Governors,
photographed in 1966 after Martin refused
to heed Johnson's plea to lower interest
rates. Many observers called the
confrontation "the Fed's finest hour."
(United Press International Photo)

4
Financing the War in Vietnam

Most of the inflationary periods in the United States have been associated with wars: the American Revolution, the Civil War, the First World War, the Korean War, and the Vietnam War. Politicians tend to be reluctant to raise taxes to cover unanticipated increases in government spending during wartime, partially because it is extremely costly to renegotiate the tax structure. In situations like this, legislation to raise taxes becomes a vehicle for tax reform as each member of Congress tries to pile on special amendments to help their constituents, hoping that the urgency of tax changes will reduce opposition to their special-interest riders.

The failure of the U.S. government to deal honestly with the costs of financing the war in Vietnam fits this overall theory of political behavior perfectly. President Lyndon Johnson feared that if he confronted Congress with a tax proposal designed to cover the increased expenditures for the war in Indochina, Congress would respond by slashing the appropriations for his Great Society programs. As a result, the necessary tax increases were postponed until 1968, by which time the unified budget deficit had soared from $1.6 billion a year in 1965 to more than $25 billion in 1968. Even when he did ask Congress for a tax increase, it took 16 months to pass the 1969 tax surcharge. Much of the delay was due to political struggles over the precise form the tax increase was to take.

Inflation was not the inevitable product of the government deficit, however. Inflation occurred because the Federal Reserve decided to finance the deficit by monetary expansion. After increasing at an annual rate of about 6 percent for 1961 to 1964, the broadly defined money supply (M_2) accelerated to a 9.5 percent rate during 1965. This acceleration in the growth of the money supply occurred at a time when the economy was operating very close to capacity. When the money supply increases rapidly and output cannot increase very much because the economy is already producing at capacity, prices must rise. This is the classic case of "demand-pull" inflation. After increasing at a rate of only 1.2 percent from early 1961 to the end of 1964, prices were rising at an annual rate of 3.5 percent by early 1966.

In 1966, the Federal Reserve briefly refrained from expanding the money supply despite the soaring deficit. In December 1965, the Federal Reserve Open Market Committee, concerned about the emerging inflation, signaled a shift to a more restrictive monetary policy by raising the discount rate from 4 to 4.5 percent despite the objections of the Johnson administration. Lyndon Johnson, who had long opposed high interest rates, took the move by the Fed as a personal affront. President Johnson immediately called William McChesney Martin (the chairman of the Fed's Board of Governors at that time) to Texas, where both the president and Treasury Secretary Fowler told Martin that they strongly opposed the Fed's action. Many observers called this confrontation "the Fed's finest hour" because Martin refused to heed President Johnson's emphatic plea for lower interest rates. The Federal Reserve succeeded in reducing the growth of the broadly defined money supply (M_2) to only 2 percent per year during the last three quarters of 1966. The narrowly defined money supply (M_1) actually fell. This monetary restraint brought on the 1966–67 minirecession and a moderation of inflationary pressures.

When the Fed does not help finance the government deficit . . . the Treasury must borrow from the public, preempting credit available for private borrowers.

Unfortunately, this restrictive monetary policy put severe strains on financial markets. When the Fed does not help finance the government deficit by buying bonds in open market operations, the Treasury must borrow from the public, preempting credit available for private borrowers. New issues of government securities to pay for military expenditures competed with credit demands by private borrowers for available funds. As a result, interest rates zoomed upward to the highest levels since the 1920s. High-grade corporate bond rates, for example, rose from about 4.5 percent in 1965 to over 6 percent in the autumn of 1966. Many aspiring private borrowers were simply unable to compete for funds with the U.S. Treasury.

Home building is particularly sensitive to rising interest rates because houses are among the most durable assets in the economy. When interest rates rise, houses become less valuable because their future services are discounted at a higher rate of interest. As a result, fewer houses are demanded at current prices and home building is depressed. The vulnerability of home building to rising interest rates was especially apparent during 1966. After remaining at a relatively stable level of 1.5 million units per year during 1964–65, housing starts fell dramatically during 1966. By the closing quarter of 1966, housing starts had fallen to an annual rate of 960,000, the lowest rate in 20 years. Other purchases of durable goods, such as automobiles, were also sharply curtailed.

By late 1966, the Federal Reserve became alarmed by the dislocation of capital markets resulting from rising interest rates and gave in to the Treasury's pressure for an expansionary monetary policy. One persistent motive in Federal Reserve monetary policies is the desire to insulate financial institutions from sharply rising interest rates. Most financial intermediaries, such as savings and loan associations, borrow short-term funds and lend them to individuals as long-term mortgages. An unanticipated rise in interest rates increases the cost of short-term borrowing, but the financial intermediary is stuck holding a portfolio of outstanding mortgages with a fixed yield. They can easily get into desperate circumstances because of this difference in duration of assets and liabilities. If the yield on the outstanding mortgages becomes less than the cost of borrowing short-term funds, the financial institution is threatened with insolvency. These considerations induced the Fed to turn to a highly expansionary monetary policy in late 1966.

In 1967 and 1968, the Federal Reserve purchased government securities in its open market operations causing the money supply to soar at the extremely rapid rate of 7.3 percent for M_1 and 10 percent for M_2. For a time after monetary policy became expansionary, interest rates moved lower. Unfortunately, this drop in interest rates was only temporary. Although open market purchases by the Federal Reserve can hold interest rates down over a short period, they tend to raise interest rates in the long run. Eventually, the increase in the money supply produces inflation. As soon as inflation becomes widely anticipated by borrowers and lenders, their expectations of continued inflation tend to raise interest rates.

It is often said that those individuals who owe a lot of money tend to benefit from inflation because the money they pay back to creditors is worth less than the money they borrowed. But, a windfall transfer of wealth from creditor to debtor occurs only if the inflation is unanticipated. If creditors and debtors correctly anticipate future changes in prices, interest rates will reflect the change in the purchasing power of the dollar and thus offset the effects of inflation. When higher rates of inflation are anticipated, higher rates of interest are charged for loans because creditors want to be compensated for the diminished purchasing power of the dollars repaid. Borrowers are willing to pay the higher rates of interest because the real assets they purchase with the borrowed funds are expected to appreciate in value simply because of the inflation and because they expect to repay the loans with dollars of less purchasing power.

In 1896, Yale economist Irving Fisher described this economic relationship between interest rates and the expected rate of inflation.[1] Fisher made the crucial distinction between *money* interest and *real* interest. If the price level is rising at 5 percent a year, a 6 percent rate of interest in terms of money is really a 1 percent rate of interest in terms of what money buys. Fisher theorized that the real rate of interest (that is, the rate of interest in terms of what money buys) is governed by the balance between the psychology of savers and the possibilities for investment. Market rates of interest are then equal to that real rate of interest plus an "inflation premium" to compensate for expected inflation.

Bond experts generally assume, as a rule of thumb, that the rate of interest on high-grade corporate bonds is the expected rate of inflation plus about three percentage points. Thus a 9 percent interest rate in high-grade corporate bonds is usually associated with an expected rate of inflation of about 6 percent per year. This relationship suggests that investors normally demand a real rate of return of 3 percent after taking into account the shrinkage of the dollar's purchasing power due to inflation.

As soon as creditors and debtors adjust their expectations to a higher rate of inflation, interest rates will rise to reflect the decline in the purchasing power of the dollar and thus offset the effects of inflation. But, financial securities issued in earlier periods, before the higher rate of inflation was generally anticipated, cannot be renegotiated. The actual number of dollars of annual interest paid to the owners of these bonds remains the same. Since investors will purchase these old bonds only if they earn the same rate of return as newly issued bonds, their market value must fall as interest rates rise.

Bonds, which have fixed interest or coupon rates, fluctuate in value because of changing market rates of interest. When the market rate of interest goes up, the price of a bond goes down because the market value of a bond is the sum of the future interest payments and the repayment of the principal discounted back to the present at the market rate of interest. As an example, consider an investor who purchases a 30-year bond with a coupon rate of interest of 3 percent and a face value of $1,000. This means that the bond will yield $30 of interest every year for 30 years and then the principal of $1,000 will be repaid. When market rates of interest are 3 percent, the bond will sell for its face value of $1,000 because the future interest payments and the repayment of the principal, discounted at a 3 percent interest rate, have a present value of $1,000. However, if inflationary expectations increase market rates of interest to a level of 10 percent, the future payments to the bondholder will be discounted at the higher rate of 10 percent, reducing the present value of the bond to only $340.

Financial intermediaries, such as savings and loan associations and mutual

---

[1]Irving Fisher, *Appreciation and Interest* (New York: Macmillan, 1896). Discussed in Irving Fisher, *The Theory of Interest* (New York: Macmillan, 1930).

savings banks, are particularly vulnerable to the kind of loss illustrated by the 30-year bond. This is because they take in short-term money from depositors, in effect borrowing it from those depositors, and lend these funds to homeowners in long-term mortgages. The money they lend out is committed for long periods of time, 20 to 30 years, at the rate of interest prevailing when the loan is made. So long as interest rates remain fairly stable—as they did during most of the postwar period until the late 1960s, when inflation skyrocketed—borrowing short and lending long presents no problem.

When interest rates rise to reflect expectations of higher rates of inflation, borrowing short and lending long threatens the financial solvency of these financial intermediaries. Long-term mortgages which were issued at low rates of interest, reflecting the expectations of price stability which prevailed in the 1950s and early 1960s, cannot be renegotiated to take account of the current inflation. The savings and loan associations which loaned out large sums for long terms at, say, 6 percent and now must pay 5.5 percent for deposited savings are in trouble. Their earnings are relatively fixed, but their cost of borrowing goes up rapidly as inflation accelerates.

Adding to these troubles are the legal limits which are imposed by the Federal Home Loan Bank Board on the interest rates savings and loan associates are permitted to pay to their depositors. When market rates of interest rise above this interest ceiling, many depositors simply withdraw their deposits and put their funds in other financial assets which can pay higher interest rates. Economists use the word *disintermediation* to designate this phenomenon of heavy withdrawals of deposits from financial intermediaries when market interest rates rise above the ceilings they can pay their depositors.

An unanticipated rise in the price level of 1 percent would transfer about $30 billion from creditors to debtors.

When significant amounts of deposits are withdrawn, the savings and loan associations and mutual savings banks have to sell off some of their portfolio of mortgages at discount prices far below the original amounts loaned to the homeowners. In this kind of crisis situation, there is a very serious likelihood that many financial institutions could become insolvent.

The rapid expansion of the money supply during 1967–68 (7.3 percent for M_1 and 10 percent for M_2) created an inflation that peaked at 5.75 percent during late 1968 and 1969. Interest rates rose to a post-Civil War record of 8.5 percent by early 1970. The Federal Reserve's attempt to lower interest rates in 1967 by monetizing the government deficit simply produced even higher interest rates as expectations generated by inflation encouraged borrowing and discouraged lending in nominal terms. Because of their inability to adapt quickly to increases in interest rates, financial intermediaries again had a drastic drop in earnings in 1969–70. The "easy money" policy of the Fed had only given them a temporary reprieve.

The main effect of demand-pull inflation is to redistribute wealth. Of course, this wealth transfer from creditors to debtors occurs only when inflation is unanticipated. Nevertheless, inflation is always popular with debtors because many creditors are locked into long-term assets with a fixed nominal yield. Debtors can benefit from substantial windfall gains resulting from an unanticipated increase in the rate of inflation. In 1970, for example, financial assets with a fixed nominal value or fixed nominal yield (such as bank deposits, currency, mortgages, government and corporate bonds, life insurance reserves, and pension and retirement funds) equaled about $3 trillion. An unanticipated rise in the price level of 1 percent would transfer about $30 billion from creditors to debtors. Moreover, if that unanticipated rise in the price level generates expectations of increased future inflation, the loss will be even greater because market rates of interest will tend to rise, reducing the market value of mortgages and bonds which have a fixed nominal yield and principal.

One famous instance in which a political group actively sought to create inflation for its own benefit occurred during the height of the Free Silver movement in the 1890s. Free silver supporters wanted the coinage of unlimited amounts of silver to inflate the money supply and produce rising prices. They were mostly Midwestern farmers, who owned large sums to Eastern bankers and Western silver miners. The movement grew out of frustration over a long period of deflation, during which prices had fallen at an average of 1 percent per year for 18 years, from 1879 to 1897.

The man who became chief representative for the Free Silver movement made one of the most famous speeches in the history of American oratory to the Democratic convention in 1896. William Jennings Bryan, who was editor-in-chief of the *Omaha* (Nebraska) *World Herald,* stood before 20,000 delegates at the Chicago Coliseum on a July afternoon and transfixed them with his passionate speech favoring the cause of those who were suffering from deflation.

The platform committee had written a plank favoring the coinage of silver, that plank declaring "that the act of 1873 demonetizing silver . . . has resulted in the appreciation of gold and a corresponding fall in the prices of commodities produced by the people; a heavy increase in the burdens of taxation and of all debts, public and private; the enrichment of the moneylending class at home and abroad; the prostration of industry and the impoverishment of the people."

When Bryan came before the teeming, shouting delegates, standing there with a smile, his hands clasped confidently before him, the shouts died away to a murmur and his voice rang out, rising in tone as he made his points. In the climactic final passage, he promised to "fight . . . to the uttermost" against the gold standard and ended by saying: "You shall not press down upon the brow of labor this crown of thorns, you shall not crucify mankind upon a cross of gold."

Bryan became the youngest man ever nominated by a major political party, but he lost the presidential election. Despite his defeat, the episode remains one of the most striking and clearly defined examples of controversy over monetary policy in American history.

Similar political pressures were at work in the late 1960s. Financing the war in Vietnam by increasing the money supply instead of raising conventional taxes resulted in a tremendous redistribution of wealth from creditors to debtors. The taxpayers who bear the burden of conventional taxes gained while the owners of nominally fixed assets lost. The homeowners of America with long-term mortgages and owners of consumer durables financed with debt, such as automobiles, gained substantially from inflation. The bondholders and the savings and loan associations bore most of the burden of the inflation tax. The government was able to meet its interest obligations to holders of government bonds with dollars of reduced purchasing power.

President Charles de Gaulle during a press
conference in Paris on November 27, 1967,
at which he launched a fierce attack on the
dollar and called for a return to gold as the
sole basis of international transactions.
(United Press International Photo)

5
Inflation and
the Dollar Crisis

The decision to finance the war in Vietnam by printing money soon created havoc in the foreign exchange market. The foreign exchange market is a figure of speech for an interconnected network of private and central banks which buy and sell different national monies. Foreign trade necessitates the conversion of one currency into another. For example, if Americans want to buy Scotch whiskey, they must convert their dollars into pounds, because Scotch distillers want to be paid in British currency. When Americans convert their dollars into pounds, they supply dollars to the foreign exchange market. When the British want to buy American wheat or financial securities or IBM typewriters, they demand dollars in the foreign exchange market. In order for the foreign exchange market to clear, there can be no dollars remaining unsold. The exact process by which the foreign exchange market attains equilibrium depends upon whether the governments in question maintain a fixed exchange rate or whether exchange rates are free to float.

Under a fixed exchange rate system, the supply and demand for dollars on the foreign exchange market will balance because central banks, such as the Federal Reserve, the Bank of England, or the German Bundesbank, agree to become buyers of whatever dollars are left unsold at the official exchange rate. If the public is supplying more dollars in exchange for foreign currencies than are being purchased with foreign currencies, the central banks must buy up the surplus dollars with foreign currencies, thus clearing the market. The deficit in the *official reserve transactions balance of payments* measures the extent to which central banks have had to buy or sell currencies to clear the market under a fixed exchange system. For example, if the central banks have to buy up unsold dollars at the official exchange rate, the United States would have a balance of payments deficit.

Obviously, fixed exchange rates cannot be maintained when countries have persistent differences in their inflation rates. The country with the highest inflation rate will soon be at a competitive disadvantage in world trade. The fixed exchange rate was one of the casualties of the accelerating inflation in the United States. As a result of financing the military expenditures in Vietnam by printing money, the U.S. had a more rapid expansion in the money supply than did Europe or Japan. Under fixed exchange rates, the resulting inflation seriously reduced the competitiveness of American goods in world markets. The U.S. trade balance of exports minus imports declined from a surplus of $6.8 billion in 1964 to a deficit of $2.7 billion in 1971. Imports of foreign steel, automobiles, and textiles captured increasing shares of American markets. Soaring U.S. imports were mirrored in an increase in the supply of dollars to the foreign exchange market. Conversely, as U.S. exports slowed in 1970–71, so did the demand for dollars. This excess supply of dollars made fixed exchange rates increasingly difficult to maintain.

If there had been no government intervention in foreign exchange markets, the excess supply of dollars would have caused the dollar to fall relative to other currencies. However, under the fixed exchange rate system established by a conference held in Bretton Woods, New Hampshire, in July 1944, foreign central banks were required to buy up the dollars which were in excess supply. The excess supply of dollars meant that there were insufficient buyers of dollars at the fixed exchange rates. To prevent a devaluation of the dollar, the British or French or Japanese central bank had to sell its own currency in order to buy the dollars which were in excess supply.

Central banks refuse to sacrifice their domestic goals of monetary policy to balance of payment equilibrium.

When a foreign central bank writes a check on itself to buy dollars, it puts more of its own currency into circulation. The purchase of foreign exchange by a central bank has the same expansionary effect on the country's money supply as the purchase of bonds in open market operations. Because this increase in the money supply will raise prices in, say, Germany, inflation will have been exported to Germany through the fixed exchange rate system. Of course, if this adjustment mechanism were allowed to operate, U.S. goods would no longer be priced out of world markets because the rest of the world would have the same rate of inflation. But this would also mean that other countries would simply allow the Federal Reserve to make their monetary policy. Since no country could have an independent monetary policy, their rate of inflation would be determined by the U.S. rate of inflation.

This adjustment mechanism is rarely allowed to operate, however, because central banks refuse to sacrifice their domestic goals of monetary policy to balance of payment equilibrium. Imported inflation can be prevented by offsetting the expansionary effects of the purchases of foreign exchange with the contractionary effects of open market sales of bonds. If the German Bundesbank, for example, simultaneously sells government bonds in open market operations when it purchases dollars in the foreign exchange market, the German money supply will remain unchanged. These "sterilization" policies, as they are called, insulate the money supply from the balance of payments. However, they also prevent the balance of payments from returning to equilibrium. The excess supply of dollars will persist.

The excess supply of dollars which led to the dollar crisis existed because most European and Japanese central banks decided to sterilize their purchases of dollars in the foreign exchange market. Since most of the dollars purchased by foreign central banks were used to purchase U.S. government bonds, foreign governments were, in effect, borrowing from their own citizens with open market sales of bonds to loan purchasing power to the United States. Under the Bretton Woods Agreement, foreign central banks did have the option of buying gold from the United States at $35 an ounce. Every secretary of the Treasury during this period spent part of his time in office traveling to Europe to persuade foreign central banks to purchase U.S. bonds rather than gold with their dollars. We wanted the surplus countries to lend our dollars back to us. Most of the European countries went along with American requests, but France did not.

General de Gaulle regarded the purchase of U.S. bonds to be an involuntary tax imposed on France to finance the United States' imperial military and economic activities around the world. Since he personally opposed the war in Vietnam, he felt that purchasing U.S. bonds would help to finance that war. His decision to buy gold rather than U.S. bonds also reflected growing French opposition to U.S. "takeovers" of European industry. In 1967, J. Servant-Schreiber wrote a book that became a best seller in France entitled *Le Defi Americain (The American Challenge)*[1] which warned of an economic takeover of Common Market economies by U.S. corporations. The Common Market discriminated against the importation of American goods through tariffs which were not applied to imports from other members of the Common Market. Moreover, the inflation in the United States made U.S. production more costly, and consequently, U.S. corporations had an incentive to move their production to sites inside the Common Market. De Gaulle referred to fears of American "takeovers" in his press conference of November 27, 1967, but he insisted the economic invasion by American corporations was due "not

---

[1] J. Servant-Schreiber, *Le Defi Americain* (Paris: Denoel, 1967; English translation, New York: Atheneum, 1968).

so much to the organic superiority of the U.S. as to dollar inflation that it is exporting to others under the cover of the gold standard."

De Gaulle's analysis was essentially correct. The purchase of U.S. government bonds by foreign central banks financed some of the budget deficit resulting from the war in Vietnam. Without these inflows of foreign capital, Americans would have had to purchase these government bonds, reducing the purchasing power they could otherwise have used to purchase goods and services. Similarly, the purchase of U.S. bonds by foreign central banks released loanable funds which could then be borrowed by American corporations to expand their operations both at home and abroad.

De Gaulle continued purchasing gold from the U.S. until 1968. In May of that year, Danny (Le Rouge) Cohn-Bendit led a student uprising at the Sorbonne which almost toppled the de Gaulle government. Eventually, the students were joined by workers in a general strike which succeeded in paralyzing the French economy. The wage explosion which followed completely eliminated France's cost advantage and the balance of trade surplus which resulted from it. Within a year, France had to devalue the franc by about 12 percent.

Richard Nixon dropped a bombshell on America's trading partners by imposing a 10 percent temporary surcharge on American imports as a means of pressuring these countries into accepting a devaluation of the dollar.

Fixed exchange rates finally collapsed from the stress which built up during the period of accelerating inflation in the United States. During 1970, foreign central banks had to buy $9.8 billion of unwanted dollars, and in 1971, they bought a record $29.8 billion. American products were at an increasingly serious disadvantage in world markets because the dollar was so overvalued. American producers of exports and of goods competing with imports put political pressure on the Nixon administration to do something about the loss of markets to foreign producers.

The European and Japanese governments were reluctant to let their currencies appreciate, or rise in value, too far against the dollar. European and Japanese export industries enjoyed the competitive advantage they had in the world market because of the dollar being so overvalued, and they used all the political pull they could muster to resist the revaluation of their currencies. Finally, Richard Nixon dropped a bombshell on America's trading partners by imposing a 10 percent temporary surcharge on American imports as a means of pressuring these countries into accepting a devaluation of the dollar. Nixon also announced that the United States would no longer sell gold to foreign central banks at $35 an ounce.

What finally came out of this power play was the Smithsonian agreement of December 18, 1971, under which the dollar was officially devalued by an average of 12 percent against the currencies of 14 other major industrial currencies. However, this devaluation of the dollar was not sufficient to eliminate the excess supply of dollars on the foreign exchange market.

U.S. balance of payments was still a substantial $10.4 billion during 1972. In early 1973, partly in reaction to the very rapid expansion of the money supply in the United States during 1972, private speculators sold large amounts of dollars in the foreign exchange markets. Foreign central banks purchased about $10 billion in the first three months of the year alone—compared to a deficit of $10.4 billion for the whole year of 1972—in an attempt to support the dollar. When this massive intervention failed to stabilize the dollar, even after an additional devaluation of the dollar in February, fixed exchange rates were abandoned.

Since 1973, exchange rates have generally been allowed to float. Central banks no longer have to "peg" the price of their currency to the dollar (although some intervention does still occur). Rather, the foreign exchange market is mainly cleared through changes in the exchange rate. Under a flexible, or floating, exchange rate system, an excess supply of dollars would cause the price of the dollar in terms of other currencies to fall until enough sellers were discouraged from selling, or enough buyers were encouraged to buy, to clear the market.

There is a marvelous, self-correcting mechanism in an ideal floating exchange rate system. As the price of the dollar falls, fewer pounds or marks are needed to purchase a dollar. Conversely, Americans have to pay more dollars to get marks and pounds. This depreciation of the dollar in terms of foreign currencies lowers the price of American goods and services relative to foreign goods and services. Americans will then tend to substitute goods produced at home for the more costly foreign imports as domestically produced products become better buys.

This shift in buying patterns from imports to domestic products reduces the supply of dollars to the foreign exchange market. In addition, the depreciation of the dollar stimulates the sale of American exports abroad and results in an increased demand for dollars. As the relative cost of producing internationally traded goods in the United States falls, foreign corporations will invest in the United States, further increasing the demand for dollars.

Changes in foreign exchange rates allow countries with different rates of inflation to continue to do business with each other. Suppose, for example, that U.S. prices rise by 10 percent, while the rest of the world has stable prices. Under a fixed exchange rate system, American products would rise in price both at home and abroad, while foreign produced goods would not. In order to prevent American products from being priced out of world markets, the dollar would have to be devalued. A 10 percent devaluation of the dollar would exactly offset the higher prices in the United States. American products would still be 10 percent more expensive in terms of dollars, but so would foreign products since it takes 10 percent more dollars to purchase foreign currencies. In terms of foreign currencies, the prices of American products would remain constant. Even though American products would be 10 percent more expensive in terms of dollars, it would take 10 percent less marks or pounds to purchase a dollar.

The breakup of the Bretton Woods monetary order occurred because of a shift in political forces toward increased monetary autonomy. Because it protects domestic industries from being priced out of world markets as a result of domestic inflation, the flexible exchange rate system now permits much greater freedom for national monetary policies and price levels. However, international considerations still play an important role in policymaking.

Arthur Okun, President Kennedy's chairman of the Council of Economic Advisers, in testimony before the House-Senate Joint Economic Committee February, 28, 1975. (United Press International Photo)

6
Wage-Push Inflation and Recession

In an inflationary recession, prices are not "pulled" up by excess demand created by expansionary monetary and fiscal policies. Rather, prices are "pushed" up by rising costs (although costs, of course, are prices, too). If prices are pushed up by rising costs at a time when total spending is increasing slowly, sales and output must fall, and the unemployment rate will increase. This is the reason anti-inflationary monetary and fiscal policies invariably produce a business recession. A sudden reduction in inflation requires some period of painful unemployment.

Every time governments have reduced the rate of growth in the money supply for an extended period of time, the rate of inflation has been reduced. Unfortunately, these anti-inflationary demand policies have never significantly reduced the rate of inflation without first precipitating a business recession and higher unemployment rates.

Anti-inflationary monetary policies slow the rate of total spending in the economy. Since total spending is the product of multiplying total output or production times the price level, a reduction in either of the two variables can bring spending down. Total spending can fall either through a reduction in prices or in production. In the short run, prices of labor and raw materials tend to resist downward change, keeping prices up. The more flexible variable in the short run is usually output or production. Consequently, the initial effect of anti-inflationary demand policies is to reduce output and employment rather than to reduce prices.

The very close relationship between changes in output and changes in the unemployment rate is called *Okun's Law*. Arthur Okun, one of Kennedy's economic advisors, examined the data from 1947–60 and found that during this period it took almost 4 percent growth in output each year to keep the unemployment rate constant.[1] This 4 percent growth rate was required because the labor force was increasing about 1.5 percent a year and each worker's productivity was increasing an additional 2.5 percent per year. For every percentage point that output growth falls below this 4 percent growth rate, the unemployment rate rises at the rate of about one third of a percentage point per year. Thus, an annual rate of growth in output of only 1 percent would cause the unemployment rate to rise by about one percentage point per year. If output grew at a 7 percent annual rate, the unemployment rate would fall by one percentage point per year.

Richard Nixon discovered this unfortunate aspect of anti-inflationary demand policies in 1969 and 1970. During 1969, the federal government finally made a significant effort to reduce the rate of inflation. The federal government actually achieved a budget surplus (in the unified budget) of $3.2 billion—compared to a $25.2 billion deficit in 1968. At the same time, the Federal Reserve restrained the growth rate of the M_1 money supply to a 3 percent annual rate—down from a 7.6 percent annual rate in 1967–68. These restrictive monetary and fiscal policies finally succeeded in reducing the rate of inflation in 1971 and 1972. Unfortunately, the initial effect of these anti-inflationary demand policies was to produce the recession of 1970. Wage negotiations during 1969 were based on the widely held belief that the inflation rate would continue at about 5 percent per year. Since *real wages* (wages expressed in terms of real purchasing power) typically increase by about 2.5 percent per year, reflecting the long-run increase in productivity, workers, expecting inflation rates of about 5 percent per year, demanded *money wage* increases of about 7.5 percent per year. However, as the anti-inflationary demand policies slowed the rate of total spending, these wage increases simply priced labor out of the market. Unemployment rates peaked at 6 percent in late 1970 and early 1971.

This episode clearly illustrates the role inflationary expectations play in producing cost-push inflation. After an extended period of demand-pull inflation, individuals become psychologically conditioned to expect rising prices. The general fear of continued inflation causes workers to demand wage increases to protect their earnings from expected increases in the cost of living. Thus, once an inflation has been set in motion, it acquires a momentum all its own. There is virtually no way to stop it without paying the penalty of excessive unemployment.

Unemployment is, of course, always present because of the dynamic nature of a market economy. At any moment in time, some industries are declining and laying off workers while others are expanding and hiring new workers. The workers who are laid off or quit their jobs will normally be unemployed for some time before they find new jobs. An unemployment rate of about 5 to 6 percent of the labor force is generally considered to be the normal unemployment

---

[1]Arthur Okun, "Potential GNP: Its Measurement and Significance," *1962 Proceedings of the Business and Economic Section of the American Statistical Association,* pp. 98–104.

resulting from this transfer of labor from declining to expanding industries.

When individuals become unemployed, very few of them will accept the first job offered to them unless the wage is comparable to the wage rate they expect to receive if they remain unemployed and continue to search for job offers. Jobs are always available for most unemployed workers, but many individuals will pass up those jobs which do not meet their *money* wage expectations. These expectations about the "acceptable" money wage rate are very sensitive to people's expectations about inflation. When restrictive monetary and fiscal policies slow the growth of total spending, individuals will often base their early decisions upon the false expectations of a continuation of rising prices and wages. Actual *money* wages offered by employers will rise at a slower rate than is expected by unemployed workers. As a result, individuals will tend to reject current job offers in the expectation of receiving higher money wage offers in the future. Since the underlying rate of inflation has been reduced, however, the chance is small that they will find those wage offers. As a result, workers will remain unemployed for long periods searching for unrealistic wage offers.

There is virtually no way to stop [inflation] without paying the penalty of excessive unemployment.

The length of time an unemployed individual spends searching for job offers is an important factor in determining the unemployment rate. The unemployment rate is equal to the percent of the labor force which becomes unemployed each week times the average duration of unemployment in weeks. The number of people who become unemployed each week from quits, layoffs, firings, and the stream of new entrants has been a fairly stable fraction of the labor force. Over the business cycle, layoffs move inversely with quits. During recessions, when layoffs are high, people who have jobs hesitate to quit. But, when times are better, quits rise and layoffs fall. As a result of this offsetting movement in quits and layoffs, the number of people who start job hunting every week has been a fairly constant .5 percent of the labor force. As an approximate rule of thumb, the unemployment rate is equal to this .5 percent of the labor force which becomes unemployed each week times the average duration of unemployment in weeks. An average duration of unemployment of 10 weeks, for example, is generally associated with an unemployment rate of about 5 percent. When wage offers rise slower than expected, in response to anti-inflationary monetary and fiscal policies, individuals tend to remain unemployed too long. The resulting increase in the average duration of unemployment is an important cause of rising unemployment rates. Since the flow of workers into the unemployed category has remained relatively constant, the unemployment rate will rise roughly in proportion to the increase in the average duration of unemployment. An increase in the average duration of unemployment from 10 to 16 weeks, for example, usually produces an increase in unemployment from 5 to 8 percent of the labor force.

Of course, rising average durations of unemployment will have the beneficial effect of reducing the *reservation* wage for which unemployed workers are holding out. After a long string of wage offers which are below their expectations, workers will usually begin to suspect that their expectations are too optimistic. These reductions in "expected" wage offers will reduce the "expected" return to continued search for job offers and unemployed workers will more readily accept lower wages.

Another important consideration in deciding whether or not to continue searching for job offers is the cost of remaining unemployed. Individuals must weigh the expectation of receiving higher wage offers through continued search against the cost of remaining unemployed. The higher the cost of remaining unemployed, the greater is the probability that unemployed workers will accept current wage offers and return to work.

Although motivated by humanitarian considerations, these additional unemployment benefits had the undesirable effect of increasing the unemployment rate.

Our unemployment compensation system mitigates the economic hardships of a recession by providing financial assistance to those families hurt by unemployment. Unfortunately, this financial aid also reduces the cost of remaining unemployed and, therefore, encourages unemployed workers to delay their return to work. Recent increases in the level and duration of benefits under the unemployment compensation system have contributed to an increase in the average duration of unemployment during recessions. Moreover, the duration of unemployment benefits has usually been extended during periods of high unemployment. In 1975, for example, Congress passed two measures which significantly reduced the costs of being unemployed. The Federal Supplemental Benefits Act extended unemployment compensation for eligible workers to an unprecedented 65 weeks from the previous 26 weeks. In addition, the Special Unemployment Assistance Act offered 39 weeks of benefits to workers not previously covered by unemployment compensation. Although motivated by humanitarian considerations, these additional unemployment benefits had the undesirable effect of increasing the unemployment rate. By some estimates, these two pieces of legislation added almost one percentage point to the unemployment rate by early 1976.

Cost-push inflation is often believed to result primarily from the economic power wielded by large labor unions. Upon closer inspection, however, the relationship between labor unions and inflation is more apparent than real. Less than 25 percent of the labor force is unionized in the United States. The fact that the unionized sector of the labor force is relatively small makes the threat of spontaneous inflation resulting from labor union wage policies highly improbable, because labor unions must be wary of the possible substitution of nonunion labor for union labor.

When union wages rise relative to nonunion wages, these cost differentials are eventually translated into price differentials. The prices of union-made products rise relative to the prices of nonunion products. Buyers will have an incentive to substitute the cheaper nonunion products for union-made products, decreasing the demand for products made by the unionized sector of the labor force. As a result, employment in the unionized sector of the labor force will be reduced as sales decline. Businesses will also have an incentive to substitute automated machinery for union labor if their wage demands are too high. These effects of high-wage policies on the part of labor unions will reduce the amount of employment which is available to their members.

However, the loss of employment opportunities in the unionized sector resulting from high union wages displaces workers who must then find jobs in the nonunion sector. This increased supply of labor to the nonunion sector will reduce wages there. The principal effect of labor unions is on the *wage structure,* not on the average level of wages.

Labor unions sometimes appear to be the cause of inflation, however, because of their lagged adjustment to unanticipated inflation. The cost of negotiating collective bargaining contracts discourages frequent negotiations. As a result, contracts usually set wage rates for two or three years in the future. The long duration of these contracts makes it difficult for union wages to adjust to changing rates of inflation. Unions could, of course, hedge against unanticipated changes in the rate of inflation by putting cost-of-living escalators in their contracts. So far cost-of-living escalators have played a relatively minor role in collective bargaining contracts. From 1964 to 1967, only about 2 million workers were covered by cost-of-living escalators. After several years of accelerating inflation, the level of coverage did increase to 4.3 million workers in 1972, but this still represented less than one fifth of the unionized labor force.

Because of this slower adjustment of union wages to unanticipated inflation, union wage increases usually lag behind increases in the nonunion sector when inflation is accelerating. When unions are finally able to renegotiate their contracts, many of their wage increases represent a "catch-up" to the cost of living. The following chart shows wage increases resulting from negotiated settlements and the average compensation in the nonfarm economy during the accelerating inflation of

Increases in Average Compensation per Man-Hour in the Private Nonfarm Economy and in Negotiated Settlements, 1966-71 (annual rate of percent change)

	Percent Average Compensation	Percent Negotiated Settlements
1966	6.1%	4.7%
1967	5.7	5.5
1968	7.3	6.5
1969	6.9	8.2
1970	7.0	9.1
1971*	7.5	8.4

Source: Bureau of Labor Statistics. Found in Otto Eckstein and Roger Brinner, ``The Inflationary Process in the United States,'' Joint Economic Committee, Congress of the United States, February 22, 1972.
*First .nine months.

1966 to 1970. The negotiated settlements in the unionized sector lagged behind the rest of the nonfarm labor force until 1969, when the wages of the unionized sector started to catch up again.

In 1970, aggregate demand slowed significantly in response to restrictive monetary and fiscal policies. At the same time, labor unions were negotiating catch-up wage increases. The catch-up wage increases appeared to be the cause of cost-push inflationary pressures at a time of substantial unemployment. In one sense, labor unions are responsible for producing cost-push inflation, but, in another sense, they are not. It depends upon the time framework. If the whole inflationary period from 1965 to 1970 is to be considered, labor unions played no special role in causing inflation. Nevertheless, during the recession of 1970, catch-up wage increases did temporarily contribute to the perpetuation of inflation, even after aggregate demand ceased to be a source of inflationary pressure.

Milton Friedman, who won the Nobel Pr
for Economics in 1976 for his achievemen
in the fields of consumption analysis,
monetary history and theory, and for his
demonstration of the complexity of
stabilization policy. Friedman and others
have suggested the use of indexing as an
alternative to wage and price controls.
(United Press International Photo)

7
Wage and Price Controls and the Shortages of 1973

That inflation can be advantageous for a government which exploits the revenue-increasing aspects of inflation was made clear in chapter 1. But there is a strong antipathy to permitting or encouraging inflation on the grounds that it distorts values and misleads people about the real purchasing power of money. If inflation goes on steadily, what is accepted in one decade as a good income becomes the poverty level in another. This continual readjustment of values is difficult for many people.

Once a steady rate of inflation is widely anticipated, much unemployment is necessary to bring that inflation rate down. People come to accept the idea that inflation will continue, and gradually they acquire "inflationary expectations." Once these are accepted, they become built into the cost structure. Businesses make agreements to buy raw materials and other supplies for future delivery at prices which reflect both buyers' and sellers' expectations of continued inflation. Workers also negotiate contracts which call for annual wage increases, again in the expectation of more inflation each year. Employers are locked into these contracts just as the workers are. Employers accept them because they need to have some assurance of a continued labor supply and some idea of what their future costs will be, so they can plan production and sales.

As a result of these interlinked series of commitments and agreements which embody expectations of rising prices, inflation acquires a momentum that carries it along even when circumstances change. Even a substantial cut in total spending caused by tighter monetary and fiscal policies has little short-term effect on inflation once it has gained this type of momentum. All that happens is a decline in output and an increase in unemployment.

Because of the increase in unemployment and the lost production which results from monetary restraint, many economists argue that it is better to learn to live with inflation. They believe that inflation which is fully anticipated, and thus bears no surprises, inflicts very few costs on the economy. Most of the painful transfers of wealth which are associated with inflation, such as the decrease in the purchasing power of savings accumulated for old age, are actually the result of unanticipated inflation. They argue that once individuals adjust to rising prices, no particular group in the economy is disadvantaged. On balance, the cost in higher unemployment and lost output is not worth any benefits that might be derived from reducing the rate of inflation, once that rate is fully anticipated.

This argument is difficult to refute. But there are grounds for counterargument due to the fact that a large number of contracts will continue to reflect preinflation conditions for a long time, because they cannot be renegotiated until their expiration. Moreover, even if it were somehow possible to anticipate variations in inflation with perfect accuracy, such an inflation would still tend to shorten time horizons, induce individuals to economize on cash balances, promote wasteful use of resources in beating inflation, and disrupt the economic information normally conveyed by changes in relative prices. In any case, even if an anticipated inflation is potentially less harmful than has been thought, the public still refuses to accept continued inflation as the best option available.

Inflation, even when largely anticipated, has been a serious political liability to incumbent politicians. No national political figure has yet advocated that we stop complaining and just learn to live with inflation. Instead, they have concentrated on finding ways to minimize the unemployment costs of reducing inflation.

Among the political proposals for easing the unemployment costs of anti-inflationary demand policies are public-service job programs. From the economic point of view, these proposals make very little sense because they would not significantly increase total employment. In order to finance the public-service jobs, Congress must levy taxes or borrow from the public. In either case, the public will have less income to spend on privately produced goods and services. Such a reduction in expenditures will also reduce the number of jobs created in the private sector. Public-service job programs cannot eliminate the unemployment costs of reducing inflation, but they do make sense to many politicians because they create the illusion that jobs are being created. Politicians then reap political benefits from their apparent charity as employers.

A public-employment program could create more jobs only if it were financed by printing more money. In this situation, private spending would not be reduced, but the only way to really reduce inflation is to reduce total spending. Printing money to finance public-service employment would simply indicate that the government was abandoning its efforts to reduce inflation.

The other alternative for alleviating the unemployment cost of anti-inflation demand policies is the imposition of wage and price controls. These controls cannot be effective in situations of demand-pull inflation, although they may be effective in reducing inflationary expectations which are producing cost-push inflation in an economy with a large stock of unemployed manpower and other surplus resources. If wage and price controls are successful in speeding the adjustment of inflationary expectations to a lower rate of inflation, the adverse employment effects may be avoided.

Terrific pressures favoring the imposition of wage and price controls built up in 1970. Despite a significant reduction in the growth rate of total spending due to a restrictive monetary policy in 1969, inflationary expectations kept prices rising at a rapid rate. Since inflation continued in the face of a decline in the growth of total spending, production declined, and the unemployment rate rose from less than 4 percent at the end of 1969 to 6 percent by the end of 1970. By late 1970, even Arthur Burns, the chairman of the Federal Reserve Board, suggested that the president create a high level wage and price review board to investigate wage and price changes. President Nixon finally gave in to these political pressures on August 15, 1971 and imposed a 90-day wage and price freeze followed by a slightly less restrictive control program during 1972 and 1973.

Public-service job programs cannot eliminate the unemployment costs of reducing inflation, but they do make sense to many politicians because they create the illusion that jobs are being created.

U.S. experience with these wage and price controls shows that they do have a significant, although temporary, effect in reducing inflationary expectations. With the exception of farm prices, which were exempt from controls, the rate of price increase declined sharply. After rising at an annual rate of 4.3 percent from December 1970 to August 1971, nonfarm prices rose at an annual rate of only 1.2 percent during the freeze. Nonfarm prices did briefly accelerate to a 3.6 percent annual rate right after the freeze, but then they decelerated again to only a 1.5 percent annual rate during the Phase II controls from February 1972 to December 1972.

Wage and price controls cannot be judged a success, however, if their effects on inflation are merely temporary. Sooner or later, controls have to be lifted if the economy is to function efficiently. In a controlled economy, prices cease to provide producers and consumers with the appropriate signals. The price system in a free market economy provides incentives to allocate resources efficiently. Even when the general price level is relatively constant, individual prices change considerably, as some prices increase and some fall. These changes in relative prices alert producers to an increase or decline in demand for specific products, inducing them to shift resources out of the production of some goods so that they can increase the production of other items which consumers have come to prefer. Changes in relative prices also provide incentives for consumers to substitute products which are in abundant supply for scarcer products. When prices are controlled, they cease to provide appropriate signals to producers and consumers and cause distortions in the allocation of resources.

Price ceilings that are effective in lowering prices simultaneously reduce the supply of the product, artificially stimulate demand, and cause widespread shortages. Price controls cause especially serious supply problems when unforeseen changes in production costs cannot be passed on to consumers. For example, many industries use internationally traded raw materials whose prices are determined in world markets. Price controls obviously cannot determine the prices of these raw materials. If these raw material costs suddenly increase and the costs cannot be passed along to consumers, producers will cut production. For example, during the 1973 ceiling on steel prices, the cost of scrap steel, whose price is determined in world markets, went up sharply. As a result, many lines of steel products were cut or discontinued, and production bottlenecks occurred in many other industries which use steel.

The difficulties of administering any wage and price control program make it clear that the likelihood of success is limited by the complexity of the price system. Government bureaucrats find it practically impossible to know what relative price structure is correct for millions of products and services at each moment in time, especially since their decisions must always appear politically sound. Any control program which obviously appears to adversely affect some groups and favor others is unlikely to achieve compliance. Moreover, mention has not even been made of the tremendous costs of the manpower, resources, and time needed to comply with such a program. The Cost of Living Council, the Pay Board, and the Price Commission cost American taxpayers about $80 million during 1973. But this expense was small compared with the costs to business of making out the forms and reports and hiring legal staffs to check them over to see that the regulations were being followed.

Wage and price control programs usually appear to be successful for about 18 months. Then the costs of the distortions and shortages introduced by controls outweigh the advantage of reduced inflationary expectations. At this point, the controls actually become a source of inflation as the bottlenecks caused by shortages of specific products curtail production.

However, a price control program is not easy to dismantle once it is in place. Just as the imposition of controls can moderate inflationary expectations, the removal of controls does the opposite. Since people see the removal of controls as "taking the lid off prices," this often causes an upward price explosion. This creates an "exit problem" for governments which have imposed temporary wage and price controls. The public becomes conditioned to attributing the success in inflation to the controls, which are so highly visible, rather than to the restrictive monetary and fiscal policies which are the real cause. Their reaction when the controls are removed is, naturally enough, to expect a resumption of inflation.

This is precisely what happened when the controls imposed by Nixon were lifted in 1974. The consumer price index, which went from an increase of only 3.3 percent during 1972 to 6.2 percent in 1973, went to 11 percent in 1974.

All in all, the risks associated with wage and price controls seem to greatly outweigh the presumed benefits. The most serious danger is that controls will be used as a substitute for responsible monetary and fiscal policies. If the money supply is expanding rapidly, wage and price controls cannot prevent inflation; but they can create widespread shortages. The exceptionally rapid growth in the money supply in 1972 assured us of the shortages experienced in 1973. The inflationary effects of this extraordinary monetary stimulus could only be suppressed temporarily by wage and price controls. The shortages of steel, paper, beef, pork, fertilizer, gasoline, and dozens of other products during 1973 were the direct economic consequence of price controls.

Milton Friedman and others have suggested the use of indexing wage contracts, as an alternative to wage and price controls, to speed the adjustment of cost structures to a lower rate of inflation. Indexation makes this adjustment automatic and immediate, avoiding the delay required when people must, first, realize that costs are rising less rapidly and then go through a psychological adaptation to that realization. If wages are tied to a cost-of-living index in collective bargaining agreements, wage costs will automatically moderate as inflation is reduced. Cost-of-living escalator clauses are becoming widespread. During the period 1964–67, only about 2 million workers were covered by the cost of living escalators, but after the experience with accelerating inflation from 1967 to 1971, the level of coverage increased to 4.3 million workers in 1972. Indexing, with its special virtue of working downward as well as upward, can speed the reduction in wage rates when the rate of inflation diminishes, and by so doing can help reduce the unemployment costs of restrictive monetary and fiscal policies.

...ortages eventually created by President Nixon's wage and price controls ...re shortage of gasoline supplies. Here a gas station near Pittsfield, ...husetts, practiced the ultimate in gasoline rationing in February, 1974. ...ted Press International Photo)

8
Richard Nixon and the Fateful 1972 Election

The significant difference between the short- and long-run effects of an increase in the money supply was discussed in chapter 3. An increase in the rate of monetary growth will usually stimulate output and employment in the short run. This happens because money wage rates and raw material costs tend to be relatively rigid in the short run. Long-term contracts to supply labor or raw materials base their prices on expectations of inflation. If the rate of monetary growth unexpectedly increases, the prices of finished goods rise relative to wage and raw materials costs, and producers will have an incentive to increase employment and output. Most of the increase in income associated with an increase in the rate of monetary growth will take the form of an increase in output and employment rather than an increase in prices.

In the long run, however, changes in the rate of monetary growth will have very little effect on output because individuals will adjust their expectations of inflation to reality. Any increase in the rate of monetary growth will ultimately increase the rate of inflation.

Most voters are unaware of the long-run consequences of monetary and fiscal policies. Nevertheless, they are aware of current economic conditions and dislike inflation and unemployment. Past elections indicate that low rates of inflation and rising output in the year before a presidential election are crucial to the political success of incumbent presidential administrations. This evidence indicates that individuals are extremely short-sighted with respect to the consequences of an acceleration in monetary growth. They tend to favor incumbents who produce a temporary spurt in output growth in election years and to overlook the long-run inflationary consequences. This myopia on the part of voters creates an incentive for politicians to manipulate monetary policy in order to produce a concurrence of the long-run effects of monetary restraint and the short-run effects of monetary expansion just before presidential elections. In the early years of an incumbent's term, monetary policy should be directed toward reducing the rate of monetary growth. In the short run, this reduced rate of monetary growth will cause some unemployment. But, in the long run, it will also reduce inflation. By the end of the four-year term, inflation rates will be lower and wage and raw material costs will reflect reduced expectations of inflation. About 18 months before the election, the rate of monetary growth should accelerate, producing rapid increases in output in the year before the election. The inflationary consequences of this monetary acceleration will only show up after the election. The U.S. elections of 1948, 1952, 1956 (a borderline case), 1964, and 1972 had this basic pattern of unemployment rates and inflation. The elections of 1960 and 1968, which do not fit this pattern, were years in which incumbents lost.

In 1964, Lyndon Johnson inherited an economy with very little inflation and an unemployment rate of about 5 percent. According to this hypothesis of political behavior, he should have taken steps to reduce the rate of monetary growth in 1965. Unfortunately the war in Vietnam disrupted Johnson's game plan. With the exception of a brief pause in 1966, the rate of monetary growth accelerated throughout his four-year term. Since the unemployment rate had already reached the "full employment" level of 4 percent in early 1966, very little further reduction in the unemployment rate was possible. Inflation accelerated from 1.2 percent in 1964 to 4.7 percent in 1968. By 1968, instead of stimulating the economy, Johnson had to ask for higher taxes in an election year to fight inflation. He ultimately decided not to seek reelection, and Richard Nixon became president by narrowly defeating the vice president, Hubert Humphrey.

Another exception to the general pattern of unemployment rates and inflation occurred in 1960. The recovery from the 1957–58 recession had barely started to pick up momentum when the Federal Reserve, then under Chairman William McChesney Martin (a Democrat), violently slowed the rate of monetary growth. After increasing at an annual rate of more than 4 percent from the summer of 1958 until the summer of 1959, the money supply actually fell at an annual rate of more than 2 percent from the summer of 1959 to the summer of 1960. The recovery from the 1957–58 recession was thus thwarted, and the country reentered a recession before it had recovered from the previous one.

Although the Eisenhower administration economists expressed little concern over the deteriorating economy, Richard Nixon's economic advisor, Arthur Burns, warned Nixon that the Federal Reserve's monetary policy would result in a recession in 1960 which could seriously jeopardize his chances of being elected president. Besides teaching at Columbia University, Arthur Burns was the expert on business cycles at the National Bureau of Economic Research. His experience as chairman of the Council of Economic Advisors in the Eisenhower administration from 1953 to 1956 had convinced him of the political importance of economic prosperity in election years.

Arthur Burns' prediction turned out to be accurate. Real output fell at an annual rate of 1.5 percent from the first to the fourth quarter of 1960. The unemployment rate rose from about 5 percent at the beginning of 1960 to over 6 percent by election day. Nixon's opponent, John F. Kennedy, concentrated his campaign on the economic issues of growth and employment. The Democratic campaign platform came out flatly for a 5 percent growth rate for output. In the final days of the campaign, these economic issues became decisive as the apparent softness of the economy created fears of recession. When election day arrived, the country was in the midst of the 26th full-fledged recession in U.S. history and John Kennedy squeaked into the presidency by a narrow margin.

With this painful lesson behind him, it is not surprising that Richard Nixon took actions to assure his 1972 reelection chances would not be threatened by high unemployment rates or inflation. Just as the hypothesized model of political behavior requires, this president immediately took steps to fight inflation early in his first term. The federal budget achieved a surplus of $3.2 billion as a result of the 1968 tax increase, and the Federal Reserve, still under William McChesney Martin, reduced the growth in the money supply (M_1) to 3 percent in 1969—down from 7.6 percent in 1967–68. Of course, in the short run, these restrictive monetary and fiscal policies increased the unemployment rate from 3.4 percent in late 1968 to over 6 percent in late 1970, but they did set the stage for much lower rates of inflation in 1971–72. The monetary restraint was timed so that the long-run effects on inflation rates would begin to emerge prior to the election.

The second phase of the game plan was to switch to expansionary monetary and fiscal policies in 1971. To make sure that the Federal Reserve did not foul up his reelection chances, Nixon appointed his friend Arthur Burns as chairman of the Federal Reserve Board of Governors in 1970. On August 15, 1971, Nixon announced his new economic policy which proposed an expansionary fiscal policy to stimulate the economy and wage and price controls to keep a lid on inflation. The Federal Reserve, now under Arthur Burns, accommodated Nixon's expansionary fiscal policies, causing the money supply (M_1) to increase by 8.2 percent in 1972 (M_2 increased by 11 percent). The economic program unfolded as planned, and the economy was booming on election day. Unemployment rates fell from 6 percent at the end of 1971 to 5.2 percent in November 1972. At the same time, inflation also moderated. In 1968, the year Nixon became president, the cost of living went up 4.7 percent. The rate of inflation accelerated to 6 percent in 1969. Nevertheless, the long-run effects of monetary restraint in 1969, combined with wage and price controls, held the rise in consumer prices to only 3.4 percent in 1972.

Richard Nixon's game plan for the 1972 election worked perfectly. Nixon was elected by one of the biggest majorities in voting history, crushing his opponent, Senator George McGovern, by a margin of 61 to 38 percent. But, in retrospect, Nixon and the country paid dearly for that majority. The economic cost of Nixon's game plan was the inflation of 1973–74.

Oil ministers at the opening of the 48th meeting of the Organization of Petroleum Exporting Countries. (United Press International Photo)

9
Food and Energy Prices and the 1974-75 Recession

Accelerations in the rate of monetary growth are usually reflected in higher rates of inflation about two years later. The 1973 inflation had its origins in the rapid growth of the money supply in 1971–72. The government budget went deeper into the red with staggering deficits of more than $23 billion in each of those years. Monetary growth became extremely expansive with M_1 increasing at a rapid 8.6 percent annual rate from January 1972 to mid-1973. This exceptionally rapid rate of monetary growth set the stage for an upsurge in inflation to about 7 percent in 1973 from only 3.4 percent in 1972. However, no one expected that prices would rise as drastically as they did.

This dramatic upsurge in inflation began in late 1972, when a change in ocean currents caused a drastic drop in the Peruvian anchovy catch to only one tenth of the normal catch (anchovies are manufactured into high protein fish meal which is used as feed for livestock). Then there were crop failures and droughts in Asia, Russia, and the Sahara. The USSR had one of the most severe droughts in recent history. Worldwide production of grains fell more than 3 percent from the previous year. These crop failures led to massive purchases of U.S. food stocks. The USSR alone contracted to buy 15 million tons of wheat and 6 million tons of feed grains.

The devaluation of the dollar in the spring of 1973 also made it easier for foreign countries to buy American food. This unexpected increase in export demand caused farm prices to rise drastically as exports competed with domestic consumption for available food stocks. From December 1972 to September 1973, the average price of farm products rose 46 percent and the average price of grains, 68 percent.

Just as food prices were beginning to level off in late 1973, the Arab-Israeli

War prompted an embargo on Arab crude oil supplies to the U.S. The embargo ended in March 1974, but the price of foreign crude oil quadrupled from a little more than $3 a barrel in early 1973 to almost $12. Gasoline, which had cost 25¢ a gallon (excluding state and federal excise taxes) in January 1973 soared to 43¢ a gallon by July 1974. These sudden jumps in the price of petroleum products also bid up the price of alternative sources of energy, such as coal and electricity.

This explosive rise in food and energy prices made monetary policy decisions extremely difficult in 1973–74. As discussed in chapter 2, total spending on domestic output (GNP) is determined primarily by the money supply. The equilibrium level of total income is that which makes the demand for money equal to the money supply. Unless the money supply increases, the rise in food and energy prices cannot affect the equilibrium level of total income derived from the sale of domestic output. Since demand for domestic food and energy products increases as a result of foreign crop failures and higher foreign crude oil prices, total spending on these products will increase. But this increases the incomes of domestic food and energy producers and thus increases their demand for money. Unless the money supply increases, there will be excess demand for money which will cause a flow disequilibrium between production and total spending. Individuals in the aggregate will not be willing to purchase all the output currently being produced. Since this excess demand for money will only partially offset the initial increase in spending on domestic food and energy products, the drop-off in sales will be concentrated in the nonfood and nonenergy industries. As producers of these products lower prices or reduce production, their incomes will fall. Monetary equilibrium is reestablished when the increased incomes of domestic food and energy producers are completely offset by a fall in the incomes of producers of other products. If total spending on domestic output is to remain the same, an increase in expenditures on domestic food and energy products must imply that expenditures on other goods must decline.

Full employment can exist only when workers accept the fact that crop failures and OPEC oil cartels have made them poorer.

When the money supply and total spending remain constant in the face of rising food and energy prices, the prices of other products must fall or sales will drop. This means that money wage rates in the nonenergy and nonfood industries must fall if full employment is to be maintained. In a world of flexible wages and prices, a rise in food and energy prices would have very little effect on the overall price level, for the prices of other goods would fall. Money wage rates in those industries must also fall in proportion to prices in order to keep the labor force profitably employed. However, if workers resist that reduction in money wage rates, employers will lay off workers and production will be cut back. If money wage rates cannot fall, keeping the money supply constant in the face of rising food and energy prices will create unemployment.

The Federal Reserve could, of course, accommodate the rise in food and energy prices by increasing the money supply. Total expenditures on domestic output could be allowed to rise with expenditures on domestically produced food and energy products, leaving expenditures on other products unchanged. Prices and wages in those industries would not have to fall in order to maintain full employment. However, since the overall price level would rise, the real wage rate of workers in those industries would still fall.

Whether adjustment occurs by falling money wage rates or rising prices in the face of fixed money wages, the relative scarcity of food and energy products necessitates a fall in the real wages of workers in other industries if full employment is to be maintained. An increase in the money supply can prevent unemployment by reducing real wage rates through inflation only if workers do not think in real terms. It is more likely that workers, discovering that the purchasing power of their money wages is being eroded by rising food and energy prices, will attempt to regain their lost purchasing power with demands for higher money wage rates. Moreover, many wage contracts are indexed to the consumer price index so that an increase in the overall price level would automatically raise money wage rates. In this sort of environment, even expansionary monetary policies cannot prevent unemployment. Full employment can exist only when workers accept the fact that crop failures and OPEC (Organization of Petroleum Exporting Countries) oil cartels have made them poorer. Any attempt to avoid that reduction in real wages will result in unemployment.

". . . the ultimate consequence of inflation could well be a significant decline in economic and political freedom for the American people." (Arthur Burns, Wall Street Journal, May 1974)

Some of the acceleration in the 1973–74 rate of inflation was certainly due to the excessive expansion in the money supply during 1972. However, one can hardly blame the Federal Reserve for the poor grain harvests, the shortage of fish meal, and the quadrupling of world oil prices. If it had not been for these special supply factors, the rate of inflation resulting from the earlier monetary growth would have been something like 7 percent. Instead, prices increased at an incredible 11.4

percent rate during 1974. In other words, less than two thirds of 1974's double-digit inflation was caused by excessive monetary growth.

The Federal Reserve refused to validate that double-digit inflation by allowing the money supply to grow fast enough to accommodate both inflation and real growth in output. The money supply (M_1) increased by only 5.7 percent from the second quarter of 1973 to the second quarter of 1974. Prices increased by 9 percent during that time period. With prices rising faster than the rate of monetary growth, a recession was guaranteed.

During 1974, many economists urged the Federal Reserve to increase the money supply at a rate slightly faster than the rate of inflation in order to prevent the recession from becoming even deeper. Nevertheless, Arthur Burns adamantly refused to accommodate double-digit inflation. In May 1974, Arthur Burns declared that "The future of our country is in jeopardy" if the rate of inflation is not moderated. With allusions to the German hyperinflation of 1921–23, Burns predicted: "Inflation at anything like the present rate would threaten the very foundations of our society. I do not believe I exaggerate in saying that the ultimate consequence of inflation could well be a significant decline in economic and political freedom for the American people." *(Wall Street Journal.)*

Shortly thereafter, the Federal Reserve reduced the rate of monetary growth. In the seven months from June 1974 to January 1975, M_1 grew at only a 1.3 percent annual rate. Since prices rose at a 10.5 percent rate during the third and fourth quarter, production fell at the fastest rate recorded since quarterly data were started in 1947. As a result, the economy plunged into the worst recession since the 1930s. This restrictive monetary policy did produce a dramatic slowdown in the rate of inflation, however. By the last quarter of 1976, the consumer price index had increased at an annual rate of only 4.2 percent.

Arthur Burns, as chairman of the Federal
Reserve Board, appeared before the Senate
Banking Committee in Washington
November 9, 1977. He said his alleged fight
with the White House over monetary policy
and the economy is journalistic
imagination. "I'm not aware of any
confrontation," he said. President Carter
named G. William Miller as Burns'
successor in December.   (United Press
International Photo)

10
The Carter-Burns Debate over Monetary Policy and Its International Repercussions

President Gerald Ford and his Council of Economic Advisors under Alan Greenspan rejected the political expediency of rapid monetary expansion during the 1976 election. Although the rate of monetary growth did accelerate from the extremely restrictive monetary policy pursued in late 1974, it still represented a fairly modest growth rate for an election year. From the first quarter of 1975 through the third quarter of 1976, the M_1 money supply increased at an annual rate of only 5.3 percent, far lower than the 8.2 percent increase during the 1972 election year.

This monetary restraint was also partially due to Arthur Burns' determination not to be accused a second time of pumping up the money supply to reelect a Republican incumbent.

In some respects, the 1976 election resembled the 1960 election. A Republican incumbent administration failed to produce rapid economic growth through monetary stimulus during the election year. Real output increased only 4.5 percent during 1976, which was quite moderate considering that the unemployment rate averaged about 7.8 percent. The Democratic opposition argued for more stimulative policies to return the economy to full employment, and like the 1960 election, the Democratic candidate won by a very narrow margin.

The relationship between President Jimmy Carter and the Republican chairman of the Federal Reserve Board, Arthur Burns, became extremely strained early in Carter's first year in office. Carter had campaigned on a platform that made a reduction in the unemployment rate its number one priority. Arthur Burns, on the other hand, preached monetary restraint which would postpone any reduction in the unemployment rate. This dispute between Arthur Burns and President Carter over monetary policy eventually led to Burns' replacement. When Arthur Burns' term as chairman of the Federal Reserve Board ended on January 31, 1978, Jimmy Carter made it clear that he wanted a radically new direction for monetary policy by appointing G. William Miller, the president of Textron, to be the new chairman. Miller acknowledged in his confirmation hearings before the United States Senate that he shared President Carter's plan for economic expansion through stimulative monetary policies.

Although Arthur Burns preached monetary restraint, in practice he had let Carter have an expansionary monetary policy. From the third quarter of 1976 to the third quarter of 1978, the M_1 money supply accelerated to an annual rate of 8 percent. By the time G. William Miller was confirmed in April 1978, the inflationary consequences of this rapid monetary expansion were already apparent. During the second quarter of 1978, the rate of inflation had accelerated to double-digit levels.

Carter's determination to pursue an expansionary economic policy so early in his term as president turned out to be a political mistake. William Nordhaus' theory of the "political business cycle"[1] maintains that a president should pursue a restrictive monetary policy early in his term. Since an acceleration in the rate of monetary growth produces an acceleration in the rate of inflation about two years later, a president should delay turning to a stimulative acceleration in the rate of monetary growth until the last 18 months before the election. By that time, the inflationary consequences of the monetary expansion can be postponed until after the election. Although William Nordhaus was appointed to Carter's Council of Economic Advisors, Carter clearly did not follow the timing of Nordhaus' theory of the political business cycle.

The acceleration of the money supply to 8 percent in late 1976 produced dramatic international repercussions. Foreign investors and multinational corporations are fully aware that a rapid growth in the money supply will produce inflation. If interest rates are not high enough to compensate these investors for the deteriorating purchasing power of dollar-denominated assets, they will look elsewhere for foreign assets yielding a higher real rate of return. For example, short-term interest rates in the United States averaged about 5.25 percent during 1977. With an increase in consumer prices of over 7.4 percent per year from the first quarter of 1977 to the second quarter of 1978, the real rate of return on those financial securities was a -2.15 percent. But, during this same period, investors could get a 1.5 percent real rate of return in Japan and 1.1 percent real rate of return in Germany on similar short-term securities.

Convinced that the Carter administration was committed to an inflationary monetary policy, the international financial community began to unload the dollar

[1]William Nordhaus, *Ibid.*

assets they held and transfer the funds to other countries, such as Japan, Germany, and Switzerland. Net capital inflows into the United States (excluding estimated exchange rate intervention by the central banks of the industrial countries) were $800 million in the third quarter of 1976. After the growth of the money supply accelerated during the fourth quarter of 1976, these capital inflows were reversed. From the fourth quarter of 1976 to the third quarter of 1977, capital flowed out of the United States at a rate of about $5 billion a quarter. These capital outflows increased to about $13.7 billion a quarter when Carter made his dispute with Arthur Burns public and named G. William Miller as his successor.

When these investors sell their dollar assets, they must convert dollars into foreign exchange in order to acquire foreign financial securities. This transaction supplies dollars to the foreign exchange market and creates a demand for foreign currencies. The magnitude of these capital outflows from the United States created excess supply of dollars at the existing exchange rate, and the dollar plunged in value. From the fourth quarter of 1976 to October 1978, the dollar fell 47 percent against the Japanese yen and the Swiss franc and 27 percent against the German mark. This dramatic fall in the value of the dollar on foreign exchange markets occurred despite massive purchases of dollars by the German Bundesbank, the Swiss National Bank, and the Bank of Japan. From the fourth quarter of 1976 to the third quarter of 1977, foreign central banks of the industrial countries purchased approximately $5 billion per quarter. This support of the dollar increased during the fourth quarter of 1977 and the first quarter of 1978 when these central banks purchased over $13.5 billion per quarter. Even this massive intervention by foreign central banks could not prevent the sharp decline of the dollar.

From the fourth quarter of 1976 to the third quarter of 1977, capital flowed out of the United States at a rate of about $5 billion a quarter. These capital outflows increased to about $13.7 billion a quarter when Carter made his dispute with Arthur Burns public and named G. William Miller as his successor.

Purchases of dollars by foreign central banks tend to inflate the money supplies of Germany, Japan, and Switzerland, unless they are sterilized by an offsetting contraction in domestic credit. The purchase of dollars are paid for with newly created marks, yen, and Swiss francs. In order to prevent an increase in their money supplies, central banks must remove these additional reserves from the banking sector through the sale of bonds or a reduction in outstanding loans to commercial banks. However, the evidence indicates that dollar purchases were only partially sterilized, because all three countries have shown an acceleration in their rates of monetary growth since the fourth quarter of 1976. After increasing at a 6.5 percent annual rate from the fourth quarter of 1975 to the fourth quarter of 1976, the German money supply has accelerated to a 12.1 percent annual rate from the fourth quarter of 1976 to the second quarter of 1978. The Japanese money supply has grown at an 11.6 percent rate from the second quarter of 1977 to the second quarter of 1978. Although the Swiss money supply maintained an exceptionally slow growth of 2 percent from the fourth quarter of 1976 to the fourth quarter of 1977, it exploded to a 33.9 percent annual rate during the first quarter of 1978. This acceleration in the rate of monetary growth will generate inflationary pressures in those countries by late 1979 or 1980.

The decline of the dollar on foreign exchange markets has had important effects on the pattern of international trade. Suddenly American producers have increased their competitive advantage in world markets. From the end of 1976 to August 1978, wage rates rose about 13.1 percent in Japan. After adjusting for the 43 percent fall in the value of the dollar in terms of yen, Japanese wage rates increased by 56.7 percent in terms of dollars. Even German wage rates went up about 26.5 percent in terms of dollars. Meanwhile, U.S. wage rates went up only 13.6 percent during this period. Given this dramatic increase in labor costs, foreign production can remain profitable only if it increases in price in terms of dollars. Since the availability of imports limits the prices that domestic producers can charge for their products, the increase in the dollar price of imports allows U.S. producers of steel, textiles, aluminum, and automobiles to raise their prices. The relative cost advantage of U.S. producers allows them to capture a larger share of the American market. Even though the increase in the price of these products induces consumers to reduce their purchases, the demand for U.S. production increases because imports fall.

Similarly, the relative cost advantage of U.S. exporters will allow them to increase their market shares of foreign markets. However, these increases in the volume of exports and decreases in the volume of imports take time to materialize. During 1978, the volume of exports did increase much faster than the volume of imports. But, the dollar prices of imports also increased substantially because of the rise in labor costs abroad. Consequently, the reported U.S. trade deficit appeared to worsen during 1978 as dollar prices rose more rapidly than real volume of the trade deficit could decline. It is common for a country's trade balance to deteriorate immediately following a depreciation of its currency. But after a year or so, differences in the relative costs of production induce sufficient changes in the volume of exports and imports to dramatically improve the trade balance. This delayed improvement in the U.S. trade balance should begin to occur during 1979.

When the trade balance starts to improve, the total amount of spending by Americans on goods and services is reduced. In order for the supply and demand for dollars on the foreign exchange market to clear, the trade deficit must be balanced by a net inflow of capital. It is this capital inflow which allows the residents of a trade-deficit country to spend more than their income. As the trade deficit shrinks, so do the offsetting capital inflows (including the purchases of dollars by foreign central banks) which permits Americans to spend more than their income. This reduction in the rate of aggregate spending does not hurt American producers of importable or exportable goods because the decline in domestic consumption of these goods can be offset by a decrease in imports or an increase in exports. However, the producers of nontraded goods, such as housing and personal services, bear the brunt of any decline in total spending by residents because the demand for their products is not influenced by exports or imports. As the 1979 trade balance improved, expenditures on housing also declined.

Carter's commitment to monetary expansion in 1977–78 did have its intended effect of bringing the unemployment rate down. However, some of the credit for the reduction in the 1977–78 unemployment rate was due to the significant reduction in the duration of unemployment benefits. As discussed in chapter 6, Congress extended unemployment benefits to a maximum of 65 weeks in 1974. These benefits were reduced to a maximum of 26 weeks on January 1, 1978. As a result of this reduction in the duration of unemployment benefits, workers tended to remain unemployed for shorter durations of time, reducing unemployment. Although it is extremely difficult to accurately determine the relative contributions of an easy monetary policy and a more restrictive unemployment compensation program to the reduction in unemployment, both had significant effects. The unemployment rate fell from 7.8 percent at the end of 1976 to only 5.8 percent by October 1978.

The price of this expansionary monetary policy, however, was a 9 percent inflation rate during 1978, hardly a propitious development for the 1980 election. Like Carter, Lyndon Johnson had succeeded in bringing the unemployment rate down significantly during the first two years of his administration, but he ended up with such terrible election prospects because of inflation that this was one of the reasons he decided not to run in 1968. Thus, Carter's bias toward monetary expansion during 1977 and 1978 may come back to haunt him as well. By the summer of 1978, public opinion polls showed that many Americans considered inflation as the number one problem facing the United States.

In the autumn of 1978, Carter responded to these fears by shifting his economic priorities. The Federal Reserve under Carter's appointee, G. William Miller, responded to the administration's new commitment to bring the inflation rate down by 1980 by sharply reducing the rate of monetary growth. This monetary restraint practically guaranteed a recession in 1979, but it will ultimately have a beneficial effect in reducing the rate of inflation in 1980. Although this monetary restraint may have come too late to meet the requirements of the political business cycle, it is still possible that a short recession during 1979 followed by a recovery in 1980 will have come in time to fit President Carter's reelection needs.

Senator William Roth (R-Del.), left, and Representative Jack Kemp (R-N.Y.), talk with reporters on October 7, 1978, after the Senate defeated the Kemp-Roth plan that would have slashed taxes by $120 billion for individuals and businesses. (United Press International Photo)

11
The Taxpayer Revolt of 1978

Besides being a year of accelerating inflation and a falling dollar, 1978 was also the year of the tax revolt. California taxpayers were the first to rebel when they went to the polls on June 6, 1978, and approved, by a 2 to 1 margin, a proposal to cut property taxes 60 percent. This proposal, known as Proposition 13, suddenly caught the imagination of many American taxpayers. The movement rapidly spread to other states so that, for a time, it seemed that American voters were on the verge of staging a taxpayer revolution.

At the congressional level, Representative Jack Kemp of New York and Senator William Roth of Delaware introduced a bill which would slash personal income taxes by 30 percent and lower the corporate income tax rate from 48 to 45 percent over a three-year period. Although this bill did not pass, Representative William Steiger of Wisconsin succeeded in forcing the Carter administration to accept a cut in the capital gains tax as an amendment to its tax package because of the intensity of the "tax revolt."

The tax bill that finally passed Congress and was signed by the president lowered the maximum tax rate on capital gains from 42.5 to 28 percent and lowered the maximum rate on corporate income from 48 to 46 percent.

Many factors contribute to the emergence of antitax coalitions among voters, but the principal contributing factor to the 1978 tax movement was inflation. The U.S. tax system was designed for a world of little or no inflation. But, the high rates of inflation experienced since 1967 have seriously distorted the whole U.S. tax structure. Because of the indirect effects of inflation on the taxation of income and capital gains, the high rates of inflation during the last decade have resulted in diminished incentives to work and save.

The progressive rate structure of the personal income tax causes the tax rate on any given level of real income to increase as inflation pushes individuals into higher nominal income tax brackets. Since the earnings from work are subject to personal income taxes, but the psychic income you receive from leisure is not, an increase in tax rates reduces the cost of leisure in terms of foregone earnings. Higher tax rates reduce the marginal incentives to work so that many individuals reduce their overtime work and take longer vacations.

Other individuals may work more as tax rates increase because they are left with less real income after taxes. If an individual's income increases at the same rate as the cost of living, the *real* pretax income remains the same. However, this individual will actually be poorer in terms of aftertax income because the increased *nominal* income will be taxed at a higher rate. Consequently, this individual may try to partially make up for the loss of real spendable income by working more.

The demand for leisure depends upon both the cost of leisure in terms of foregone earnings and the individual's real spendable income. An increase in tax rates has two possible effects on work effort: a substitution effect and an income effect. The aftertax wage rate is the cost of leisure. Consequently, an increase in tax rates reduces the cost of leisure and induces individuals to reduce their work effort and consume more leisure. This is the *substitution effect.* But an increase in the income tax rate will also reduce spendable income and, therefore, the demand for leisure. This is the *income effect.* Ultimately, the resulting outcome of an increase in tax rates depends upon which of these effects is the strongest.

. . . the high rates of inflation during the last decade have resulted in diminished incentives to work and save.

During the last decade, the increase in tax rates on personal income resulting from inflation has significantly reduced work effort. For some groups, particularly the middle class, the income effects of an increase in tax rates may have outweighed the substitution effects. But for the population as a whole, there were no net income effects. The tax revenue resulting from increased tax rates has, by and large, gone to support welfare programs. These programs, which are based upon some criteria other than work, essentially transfer income from producers and workers to others. Although the real spendable income of the individuals who pay the taxes may go down, thus reducing the demand for leisure, the recipients of the income transfer have more spendable income and thus consume more leisure. In fact, some transfers, such as social security payments and unemployment compensation, actually require the recipients not to work. Such transfers obviously increase the incentive to substitute leisure for work.

In this sense, the effects of the increase in marginal tax rates during the last ten years are very different from those of previous periods of tax rate increases. Most of those periods were associated with wars. For example, tax rates went up tremendously during World War II, but this seemed to have little effect on work effort. This was because the income effects of a tax rate increase were not canceled out by transfer payments to other individuals. The tax revenues were used to acquire goods and services for the war effort, and taxpayers were indeed poorer as a result of these tax rate increases.

The taxation of income also induces individuals to "do-it-themselves" rather than specialize in those tasks in which they have a comparative advantage. By way of illustration, let us suppose we have a freelance auto mechanic and a house painter, each of whom sells their services for $15 an hour. If each of these workers is in a 33 percent marginal tax bracket, each earns $10 an hour after taxes. This means that they value their leisure to be worth $10 an hour since that is the opportunity cost of not working. If the mechanic wants to have his house painted, he can either hire the painter at $15 per hour or he can do it himself. If the painter requires 10 hours to complete the job, it will cost the mechanic $150, $50 of which will go to the government in taxes. That $150 would cost the mechanic 15 hours of work since an individual in the 33 percent marginal tax bracket must earn $225 before taxes in order to earn $150 after taxes. Alternatively, the mechanic would be willing to give up 15 hours of his leisure time valued at $10 an hour to paint the house himself. Therefore, if he can paint the house in less than 15 hours, he will do it himself rather than hire the painter. This is obviously an inefficient use of labor. Up to 5 extra hours of labor is wasted painting the house because the exchange of labor services is taxed. The higher the marginal tax rate the greater is the incentive to "do-it-yourself" in order to avoid taxes.

The effects of inflation on the accumulation of capital are even more serious than its effects on work effort. In order to accumulate capital, individuals must defer consumption, or save. This decision to save depends critically on the real rate of return individuals can receive on their savings. The American taxation system has always been biased against saving, but this distortion becomes much more destructive in the presence of inflation.

One of the most detrimental effects of inflation on incentives to save occurs because the inflation premium is taxed in nominal rates of interest. Savings and investment decisions are based upon real rates of return, that is, the nominal rate of interest adjusted for inflation. Irving Fisher pointed out many years ago that expectations of future price increases generate an inflation premium in nominal rates of interest equal to the expected rate of inflation.[1] But even if the inflation

[1]Irving Fisher, *Ibid.*

premium increases percentage point for percentage point with the rate of inflation, the real yield to investors will fall because the inflation premium is taxed as income.

In order to better illustrate this, imagine an investment project which yields a real rate of return of 4 percent. In a world of no inflation, the project can be profitably undertaken only if the firm can obtain a loan or issue a bond at 4 percent interest or less. On the other hand, if prices were expected to increase at 5 percent a year, the firm could pay up to 9 percent interest on the borrowed funds and still undertake the project because the current dollar value of the project will appreciate at the rate of inflation. The nominal yield on the project is 9 percent (the 4 percent real yield plus a 5 percent yield in nominal capital gains generated by inflation). Unfortunately, the inflation premium in the nominal interest rate is treated as taxable income. An individual in the 50 percent marginal tax bracket could buy the bond yielding 4 percent interest in a world of no inflation and receive a real rate of return of 2 percent (50 percent of 4 percent). But, in a world where prices are rising at 5 percent a year, even if an individual buys a bond yielding 9 percent, the real yield will be only a negative .5 percent (4.5 percent nominal rate of return after taxes minus the 5 percent rate of inflation).[2]

Through the taxation of nominal capital gains, inflation causes a similar distortion in aftertax rates of return to investors in common stock. In order to finance an investment project yielding a 4 percent real rate of return (after payment of corporate income taxes), a corporation could profitably issue common stock with dividend yield of up to 4 percent. In a world of no inflation, an investor in a 50 percent marginal tax bracket who purchased that common stock would receive a real rate of return of 2 percent (50 percent of 4 percent). In a world of 5 percent inflation, the individual would still receive a 2 percent real rate of return in the form of dividends so long as the price of the stock increased at the same rate as inflation. However, this increase in the price of the stock, necessary to keep the value of the stock constant in terms of purchasing power, is itself taxed as a capital gain. If the capital gains tax rate is one half of the personal income tax rate, the real rate of return to holding the stock for one year would be only .75 percent in a world of 5 percent inflation (2 percent real rate of return as a dividend minus 25 percent of the 5 percent nominal capital gain).

Additionally, since depreciation allowances are based upon historic costs rather than current replacement costs, inflation also increases the taxation of capital at the corporate level. Suppose a corporation invests in a machine that costs $100

---

[2]This example ignores the fact that the inflation premium in nominal rates of interest is deductible from the taxable income of the borrower. Since borrowers are able to shelter some of their income with this deduction, they theoretically could pass this tax savings on to lenders and thus compensate them for the taxes they pay on the inflation premium. However, U.S. data provide no evidence that this has occurred. For a discussion of this point, see Michael Darby, "The Financial and Tax Effects of Monetary Policy on Interest Rates," *Economic Inquiry,* Vol. 13 (June, 1975).

and yields a 4 percent real rate of return before taxes. In a world of no inflation, a $100 machine that lasts only one year must produce $104 of income to the corporation in order to earn a real rate of return of 4 percent. The corporation would be able to deduct $100 as depreciation and pay corporate income tax of 46 percent on the $4 net income, leaving the corporation with an aftertax return of about 2 percent. Alternatively, with the price level rising at 5 percent a year, the machine would have to produce $109 of income in one year in order to yield a 4 percent real rate of return before taxes. Even though the replacement cost of the machine has risen to $105, the depreciation for tax purposes still remains at its historic cost of $100. The corporation will have to pay taxes on $9 of net taxable income. The aftertax real rate of return to the corporation will fall to approximately a negative .14 percent (54 percent of 9 percent minus the 5 percent rate of inflation). Because depreciation allowances are based on historic costs, inflation converts the cost of recovering capital into taxable income. The corporate income tax is levied not only on the income generated by the capital, but also on the capital itself.

> **The American taxation system has always been biased against saving, but this distortion becomes much more destructive in the presence of inflation.**

By lowering the real aftertax yield to investors, inflation reduces the incentive to save and to provide funds for new investment. During the last ten years of historically high rates of inflation, the rate of capital accumulation has declined significantly. Real business fixed investment (in 1972 dollars) for each new worker added to the labor force fell from $79,000 during the period from 1950–69 to only $56,000 during the 1970–77 period. An increase in capital per worker is one of the main sources of labor productivity increases. It is, therefore, not surprising that this slowdown in the growth of capital per worker has adversely affected labor productivity. From 1950 to 1969, output per man-hours in the private, nonfarm sector increased at an annual rate of about 2.4 percent. Since 1969, this growth in output per man-hour has slowed to a little over 1.5 percent per year.

Most economists agree that a reduction in tax rates would increase the rate of economic growth through increased incentives to work and save. However, they fear that a reduction in taxes without a corresponding cut in government spending would lead to enormous budget deficits. The bill introduced by Representative Kemp and Senator Roth, designed to reduce income tax rates by one third over a three-year period, would have entailed a loss of tax revenue amounting to about $124 billion if the tax base remained the same. If the federal government were forced to borrow $124 billion to offset the loss of tax revenue, some economists fear that the resulting increase in interest rates would crowd out the very investment spending the tax cut was meant to stimulate. Any attempt by the Federal Reserve to moderate the rise in interest rates by open market purchases of bonds would simply inflate the money supply, raising the spectre of even higher rates of inflation.

Voters appear to favor a reduction in tax rates, but it is not clear that they are willing to reduce government spending. The success of Proposition 13 in California was at least partially due to the existence of a $3 billion surplus in the state budget. This made it possible to maintain the level of government spending in the face of lower tax revenue. This possibility does not exist at the federal level. The federal budget deficit was already $48.8 billion during 1978. The loss of an additional $100 billion in tax revenue would be staggering.

Economist Arthur Laffer of the University of Southern California claims that a reduction in tax rates need not give rise to a substantial budget deficit.[3] He contends that although individuals and corporations would pay taxes at a lower rate, taxes would be levied on a larger base of taxable income. The tax base would be expanded through a combination of increased production and decreased tax avoidance. So long as the reduction in marginal tax rates encourages work and saving, the resulting increase in production will obviously expand the tax base. Moreover, the incentive to avoid taxes entirely by the use of tax shelters is reduced as tax rates are reduced because avoiding taxes is a rather costly activity.

Most tax-shelter investments yield very low rates of return. They are attractive to investors only because they offer the opportunity to avoid taxes. An investor in the 70 percent marginal tax bracket would find it profitable to invest in a tax shelter yielding 6 percent tax free even if it were possible to earn a 15 percent rate of return on an unsheltered investment. If the marginal tax rate were lowered to 50 percent, however, the investor would choose the unsheltered investment and pay taxes on the 15 percent before-tax return. The individual's aftertax rate of return would increase by 1.5 percentage points, and the government would receive additional tax revenue. Moreover, society is likely to benefit because available savings would be directed to more productive investments.

It is not clear whether an increase in the tax base would completely offset the reduction in tax rates, but experience with the Kennedy tax cut of 1964 indicates that the expansion of the tax base would be substantial, especially for the higher income brackets. The highest marginal tax rate on income was 91 percent in 1963. The Kennedy tax cut lowered this ceiling rate to 77 percent in 1964 and to 70 percent in 1965 and later years. As tax rates declined, many forms of tax avoidance

[3]See A. Laffer's analysis in *Leading Economists' Views of Kemp-Roth,* U.S. Congress, House Budget Committee (August, 1978)

were no longer worth their costs. The figures collected by Michael Evans of Chase Econometrics indicate that the decline in tax avoidance resulting from the reduction in tax rates actually produced an increase in the taxes paid by wealthy investors.[4] After virtually no growth in taxes paid during the three years preceding the tax cut, taxes collected from individuals earning $1 million or more actually doubled during the two-year period following the 1964 tax cut.

Another means of tax avoidance is the deferment of the realization of capital gains. Taxation of a capital gain occurs only when the gain is realized through the sale of the asset, not when it accrues. Consequently, an investor can avoid paying the capital gains tax simply by holding on to the asset. Investors have less incentive to take advantage of current market developments because the rearrangement of their investment portfolios would force them to realize capital gains. As an example, suppose an investor purchased United Airlines' stock during 1977 at a price of $20 a share. A little over a year later, when the price of the stock had risen to $40, the investor came to the conclusion that United Airlines would under perform the market in the future. The investor would like to sell the United Airlines' stock and put the funds into other stocks which could be expected to outperform the market in the future. If the United Airline's stock is sold, however, the investor must pay capital gains taxes on the realized gains of $20 per share. If the taxes outweigh the incremental gain that could be expected from rearranging the portfolio, the investor can avoid those taxes by continuing to hold the United Airlines' stock. This incentive to defer realization of the gains tends to lock investors into appreciated assets and reduces the incentive they might otherwise have had to invest in securities with more potential for future appreciation.

Martin Feldstein and Joe Slemrod, economists at the National Bureau of Economic Research, have found strong evidence of the existence of this "locked-in effect" in the data collected for the years before and after the Capital Gains Reform Act of 1969, which raised the maximum capital gains rate from 25 percent to 42.5 percent. This increase in the maximum capital gains tax rate had little or no effect on the tax rates of individuals with incomes of less than $100,000. However, for individuals with incomes over $100,000, the act sharply increased the capital gains tax rates. One would expect to find a sharp increase in the incentive to defer the realization of capital gains in the higher-income groups. Feldstein and Slemrod compared reported capital gains of various income groups for 1969 (when capital gains were taxed at the old rates) with those for 1970 (when the new rates became effective). Individuals with incomes of less than $100,000, whose tax rates were essentially unaffected by the 1969 act, reported net capital gains for 1969 that were

⁴Michael Evans, Taxes, Inflation, and the Rich," *Wall Street Journal,* August 7, 1978.

34 percent higher than in 1970. However, in the $100,000 to 500,000 income group, net gains were 63 percent higher in 1969 than in 1970. In the over $500,000 income group, net gains reported in 1969 were 145 percent higher than those reported in 1970. The increased capital gains tax rates for the higher income groups definitely reduced the amount of capital gains realized. This evidence indicates that the increase in the maximum capital gains rate in 1970 might actually have reduced capital gains tax revenue by reducing the tax base.[5]

Such historical evidence supports the Laffer hypothesis that an expansion of the tax base will substantially offset the effects of a reduction in marginal tax rates. In addition, if the tax reductions stimulate employment and production, government spending on employment compensation and welfare payments may decline and further reduce the budget deficit resulting from a tax rate reduction.

No politician had to vote for the increase in tax rates produced by inflation.

Even if a tax rate reduction does increase the government deficit, fears that budget deficits will "crowd out" investment spending are largely misplaced. The crowding out argument is based upon presumed income or wealth effects of a switch from tax to debt finance. By way of illustrating the crowding out argument, assume that a reduction in tax rates has no effect on the tax base so that tax revenue falls by $100 billion. The government finances this loss of tax revenue by selling $100 billion of bonds to the public. Since the aftertax income of taxpayers has increased by $100 billion, they should feel wealthier and, therefore, should spend at least some of the increase in aftertax income on increased consumption. If individuals consume some of the increase in aftertax income, however, savings by individuals will increase by less than the $100 billion necessary to finance the increase in government borrowing. This gap between the increase in government borrowing and the increase in private savings must be closed by a rise in interest rates. As interest rates rise, fewer private investment projects are profitable to undertake. Since the reduction in profitable investment opportunities also reduces the demand for credit, private savings can be diverted from financing private investment projects to financing the budget deficit. This is the manner in which deficit finance crowds out private investment.

There is a fundamental weakness in this argument, because individuals are not wealthier as a result of the tax reduction. The presumed wealth effects do not exist.

[5]Martin Feldstein and Joel Slemrod, "The Lock-in Effect of the Capital Gains Tax: Some Time Series Evidence," *National Bureau of Economics Research Working Paper,* March 28, 1978.

Financing a loss of revenue by borrowing does not reduce the tax burden; it merely shifts the burden into the future. The future interest liabilities to bondholders must come from tax revenue. If government spending is expected to remain the same, lower taxes today must mean higher taxes in the future. Taxpayers who have perfect foresight with respect to the future tax liabilities implict in government borrowing would save all of the increase in their aftertax incomes resulting from the tax cut to provide for these increased tax liabilities. If taxpayers actually had such foresight, the tax rate reduction would generate $100 billion dollars of additional savings at existing interest rates, and the budget deficit could then be financed without an increase in interest rates or crowding out of private investment.

Although the recognition that budget deficits embody future tax liabilities does weaken the crowding out argument, the financing of a tax rate reduction through the sale of bonds also weakens the incentive of taxpayers to accumulate capital. If a reduction in current tax rates is expected to be offset by higher tax rates in the future, the temporary drop in tax rates will provide little or no incentive to invest in long-lived capital goods.

The tax revolt of 1978 has not, as yet, succeeded in making significant changes in the tax system, although very few political observers regard it as just a temporary aberration. The extent of the current disincentives to work and save in our tax system were unintended, since they were arbitrarily created by the current high rates of inflation. No politician had to vote for the increase in tax rates produced by inflation. Congress was delighted, however, to use the tax revenue generated by inflation to finance a tremendous increase in expenditures on social programs. Government expenditures increased at an annual rate of approximately 13.5 percent from 1974 to 1978. Since defense spending increased at an annual rate of only 8 percent during this period, nondefense expenditures soared at an annual rate of over 15 percent.

Although many Republicans, such as Representative Jack Kemp, have accepted Arthur Laffer's argument that a tax rate reduction would expand the tax base to such an extent that tax revenue would increase in the long run, most members of Congress still worry about the budget deficits that might result from a massive tax cut. However, even many liberal Democrats are now advocating a shift in emphasis to less government and lower taxes.

For the first time in many years, President Carter has proposed a budget for fiscal 1980 which calls for virtually no increase in real expenditures after adjusting for inflation. Although the proposed expenditure of $536.1 billion is hardly austere, it is only 7 percent higher than expenditures during the 1979 fiscal year. This represents a marked departure from the average increase of 13.5 percent from 1974 to 1978.

The related issues of tax reform and the limitation in spending on social programs will certainly be a major issue in the 1980 election.

Treasury Secretary Michael Blumenthal, appearing before the Senate Banking Committee on November 11, 1977, said th Federal Reserve Board's monetary policy i consistent with the administration's efforts to sustain consistent economic growth. (United Press International Photo)

12
Legislating Inflation and Unemployment

The M_1 money supply increased at an annual rate of 8 percent from the third quarter of 1976 to the third quarter of 1978. This rapid rate of monetary growth was consistent with an underlying inflation rate of about 7 percent during 1978. A substantial portion of the difference between this underlying rate of inflation and the 9 percent rate of inflation actually experienced during 1978 can be explained by several cost-push pressures on the price level. Among these were an increase in the minimum wage, the increase in social security payroll taxes, and the devaluation of the dollar.

The devaluation of the dollar is both a product of inflation and a source of cost-push inflation. As explained in chapter 10, the devaluation of the dollar initially occurred because investors expected prices to rise faster in the United States than in the rest of the world. When this happened, the dollar fell in value relative to other currencies simply to prevent American products from being priced out of world markets. If the rate of inflation is 10 percent higher in the United States than in the rest of the world, the dollar must drop in value by 10 percent per year against foreign currencies if American products are to remain competitive. In this sense, the depreciation of the dollar was basically a symptom of inflation rather than a cause.

When speculation against the dollar causes the value of the dollar to fall by more than the inflation differential between the United States and the rest of the world, it becomes a source of cost-push inflationary pressures because world demand is increased for traded goods produced in the United States. This, of course, increases their prices. This increased spending on domestically produced traded goods increases the income of domestic producers of traded goods and thus their demand for money. If the money supply does not increase to validate the increase in demand, spending on nontraded goods must decline in response to the excess demand for money. Eventually the reduced spending on nontraded goods will reduce their prices, offsetting the rise in the price of internationally traded goods. But in the short run, nontraded goods have relatively rigid prices because labor and raw material prices have been determined by prior contracts. As a result, the rise in the prices of internationally traded goods is not initially offset by a fall in the prices of nontraded goods, causing the overall price level to increase. This short-run cost-push effect of the devaluation of the dollar added approximately one percentage point to the underlying rate of inflation during 1978.

Two other sources of cost-push inflation were legislated by the federal government. On January 1, 1978, the minimum wage was increased from $2.30 an hour to $2.65, an increase of about 15 percent. On the same day, social security payroll taxes levied on both employees and employers were raised from 5.85 to 6.05 percent, and the taxable wage base was increased from $16,500 to $17,700. These two pieces of legislation caused hourly labor compensation to soar, adding about two thirds of a percentage point to the underlying rate of inflation in 1978.

Any tax which drives a wedge between employer compensation and after tax receipts will discourage work effort.

The minimum wage increase alone contributed about .45 of a percentage point to the rate of inflation in 1978. Recognizing the inflationary impact of this legislation, G. William Miller, the chairman of the Federal Reserve Board, urged Congress to postpone for two years the additional 25¢ an hour increase in the minimum wage scheduled to take place on January 1, 1979. He also recommended that Congress establish a special, lower minimum wage for teenagers. Miller argued that a deferral of the increase would make a significant contribution to reducing inflation. But Congress, responding to tremendous lobbying pressure from organized labor, did not accept his advice and the minimum wage jumped to $2.90 an hour on January 1, 1979. This action added about one third of a percentage point to the 1979 inflation rate.

Economists have generally opposed minimum wage legislation because it reduces the jobs available to unskilled workers.[1] Employers can profitably hire

[1]See, for example, Yale Brozen, "The Effect of Statutory Minimum Wages on Teenage Unemployment," *Journal of Law and Economics* (April, 1969), pp. 109–122; Thomas G. Moore, "The Effect of Minimum Wages on Teenage Unemployment Rates," *Journal of Political Economy* (July/August 1971), pp. 897–902; and Walter Williams, "Government Sanctioned Restraints that Reduce Employment Opportunities for Minorities," *Policy Review* (Fall 1977).

workers only if the extra revenue they generate for the business can cover the costs of hiring them. If low-skilled workers can increase the production of a business firm by two units an hour, and each unit can be sold for $1.15, the workers can be profitably employed only at a wage rate of $2.30 an hour or less. If the minimum wage arbitrarily increases the cost of hiring a worker to $2.65 an hour, some low-skilled workers can no longer generate enough extra revenue to the business firm to make their employment profitable. Obviously, producers cannot sufficiently raise prices to cover the increased wages of all their low-skilled workers because the higher prices will cause sales to fall.

Because of this detrimental effect on employment of unskilled workers, the minimum wage is an ineffective method of helping the poor. Those unskilled workers who are able to keep their jobs do benefit from increases in the minimum wage. But many other unskilled wage earners lose their jobs, and instead of receiving the minimum wage, they receive no wages at all. Of course, these disadvantaged workers may go on welfare or receive unemployment compensation, but even when this is taken into consideration, low-wage workers in the aggregate do not gain much from the minimum wage.

Edward Gramlich,[2] an economist at the University of Michigan, has attempted to estimate the effects of the minimum wage on the incomes of various categories of low-wage workers while taking unemployment compensation into account. He finds that teenage workers in the low-wage category clearly lose as a result of an increase in minimum wage rates because high minimum wages substantially reduce full-time employment, forcing teenagers into part-time employment or unemployment. The teenagers who become unemployed are particularly disadvantaged because they have a very low probability of qualifying for unemployment compensation. Adult males in the low-wage category break even or benefit only slightly. The employment of low-wage adult women actually increases when the minimum wage rises, but this may be due to increased financial pressures compelling homemakers to enter the labor force, particularly in families where teenagers have lost their jobs.

Because the minimum wage increases the wages of some low-wage workers at the cost of reducing the employment of other low-wage workers, it has had virtually no effect in raising their aggregate incomes. The redistribution of income which occurs as a result of an increase in the minimum wage is not from the "haves" to the "have nots," it is from some "have nots" to other "have nots." Moreover, the low-wage workers who have the most skills and the greatest productivity are the very workers who are most likely to keep their jobs. The least productive workers, and the group with the greatest degree of poverty, are the most likely to lose their jobs.

[2]Edward Gramlich, "Impact of Minimum Wages on Other Wages, Employment, and Family Incomes," *Brookings Papers on Economic Activity,* No. 2 (1976).

Despite the fact that the minimum wage has failed to raise the incomes of low-wage workers in the aggregate, it is an extremely popular piece of legislation. This is not as puzzling as it may seem. When the wages of unskilled labor rise, businesses have an incentive to substitute other factors of production, such as skilled labor for unskilled labor. Consequently, when an increase in the minimum wage raises the cost of unskilled labor, the demand for skilled workers will increase. As a simple illustration of this substitution effect, let us assume that an unskilled worker can produce a pair of shoes in four hours, while a skilled worker requires only two hours. With a minimum wage of $2.30 per hour, the labor costs of producing a pair of shoes using unskilled labor is $9.20. Skilled workers could not get more than $4.60 an hour for their labor because they would price themselves out of the market. If the minimum wage increases to $2.65 an hour, however, businesses would replace unskilled labor with skilled labor until competition for skilled workers bids their wage rates up to $5.30 an hour. The net result is a shift in demand from unskilled labor to skilled labor which raises the wages of the skilled workers.

Labor unions, whose members are generally skilled, are well aware of this substitution effect. They support minimum wage increases, not out of altruistic motives, but in an attempt to increase the costs of using substitutes, thus increasing the demand for their members. The principal beneficiaries of the minimum wage are not low-wage unskilled workers, but skilled workers who are already making more than the minimum wage.

Redistribution of income which occurs as a result of an increase in the minimum wage is not from the "haves" to the "have nots," it is from some "have nots" to other "have nots."

This same substitution effect causes shifts in the location of industry to different regions of the country. Labor intensive industries, such as textiles, canning, paper, and furniture, have an incentive to locate in low-wage regions. The minimum wage is an effective means of retarding the migration of labor intensive industries from high- to low-wage areas of the country, thus protecting workers in the high-wage areas from potential competition. Legislators from the more industrialized regions tend to be the most vocal supporters of higher minimum wages. This point was brought out very clearly by Senator Jacob Javits of New York:[3]

[3]U.S., Congress, Senate, *Congressional Record,* 2692.

I point to Senators from industrial states like my own that a minimum wage increase would also give industry in our states some measure of protection as we have too long suffered from unfair competition based on substandard wages and other labor conditions in effect in certain areas of the country—primarily in the South.

Just as an increase in the minimum wage tends to increase prices and reduce employment, so does an increase in social security payroll taxes. The recent increases in the social security payroll taxes, however, are only symptomatic of even more serious problems with the financing of the social security program. Harvard Professor Martin Feldstein contends that the pay-as-you-go method of financing social security benefits has, in and of itself, enormous long-run effects on the price level through its effects on productivity.[4] The social security program's effects on productivity are indirect but massive. Social security retirement benefits that have been promised to the current working population are a close substitute for private savings. In the absence of the social security program, the working population could provide for retirement years only by saving some of their income during their working years. In fact, provision for retirement is one of the principal motivations for saving. Since the social security benefits are a close substitute for private savings in providing for retirement, workers often reduce their personal savings. Feldstein's research seems to indicate that social security benefits reduce private provisions for retirement almost dollar for dollar. However, unlike private savings, the contributions paid to the Social Security Administration are not invested in productive assets. They are paid out directly to current retirees. If the promised social security benefits reduce the private provisions for retirement dollar for dollar, they likewise reduce the country's productive assets. That is, the unfunded liabilities of the social security program represent a reduction in the capital stock resulting from the reduction in personal savings.

In 1974, these unfunded liabilities amounted to $2.4 trillion. Since total private wealth in that year was approximately $3 trillion, this means that the capital stock was about 40 percent lower than the $5 trillion which would have existed in the absence of the social security program. This reduction in the capital stock implies that output per man-hour was reduced by as much as 14 percent. In other words, with the same money supply, output could have been 14 percent higher and prices 14 percent lower if individuals had provided for their retirement out of private savings.

Although the pay-as-you-go method of financing the social security program remains a serious long-run problem, the short-run effects of the recent increases in social security payroll taxes are of more immediate concern to politicians. The

[4]Martin Feldstein, "Social Security and America's Capital Shortage," in *The Economy in Transition,* ed. Robert C. Blattberg (New York: New York University Press, 1976).

tendency of increases in the payroll taxes to increase prices and reduce employment occurs for a number of reasons. Half of these payroll taxes are paid by the employer, and the employee pays the other half. The employer's half of the payroll tax is actually included in the cost of doing business. When these employer payroll taxes are increased, and wage rates remain the same, the increased costs are passed on to consumers in the form of higher prices. This is exactly what happened on January 1, 1978, when the employer payroll tax was increased from 5.85 to 6.05 percent and the taxable wage base was increased from $16,500 to $17,700. The increase in the tax rate added about $1.5 billion to labor costs, and the increase in the taxable wage base, an additional $1 billion. These increases in labor costs amounted to about .2 percent of total labor costs. Assuming that prices are proportional to unit labor costs, these changes in the employer payroll tax raised prices in the short run by about .2 percent.

Of course, in the long run it cannot be assumed that wages will be unaffected by the increase in payroll taxes because that depends on the long-run supply of labor. In the absence of any increase in the money supply, total employment can remain unchanged only if wages fall by an amount equal to the increased taxes paid by employers. However, important reasons exist why the supply of labor cannot be expected to remain the same. The social security payroll tax, like any other tax on wage income, introduces a wedge between the total cost of hiring a worker and the actual aftertax compensation received by the employee. This tax wedge is the sum of both the employer and the employee contributions. At the 1978 level of 6.05 percent levied on both employers and employees, the tax wedge would amount to 12.1 percent. Since this tax wedge means that the employee does not receive his or her total marginal contribution to the firm's revenue, it reduces the aftertax returns that encourage work and, therefore, subsidizes leisure at the expense of production. Even with a given money supply, the reduction in work effort and production will lead to higher prices.

From 1970 to 1975, real [social security] benefits, after accounting for inflation, increased 56 percent while real gross national product rose by only 10 percent.

Because of these inflationary consequences of the social security payroll tax, many public figures, such as Alfred Kahn (President Carter's chief inflation fighter), George Meany (president of the AFL-CIO), and even the Council on Wage and Price Stability, want Congress to reduce the payroll tax. However, secretary of the Treasury, Michael Blumenthal, has opposed any change in the increases which were scheduled to take effect because the revenue was badly needed to prevent an alarming outflow from the social security trust fund. Although this loss of revenue could be funded by an increase in personal income taxes, it would not get rid of the disincentive effect on work effort. Any tax which drives a wedge between employer compensation and aftertax receipts will discourage work effort. Even government borrowing to finance the loss of revenue from reduced payroll taxes will not solve the problem, because government borrowing necessitates higher taxes in the future to pay the interest on the government debt. Borrowing would just postpone an inevitable increase in taxes.

Although a switch from payroll taxes to personal income taxes would not eliminate the disincentive effect on work effort, it may have other desirable aspects. As Milton Friedman has pointed out, the social security payroll tax is the most regressive tax in our tax system.[5] The employee will eventually bear the employer's share of taxes as well as the employee's share because employers will either raise prices, reducing the real wages of employees, or wages will have to drop by an amount equal to the employer's share of the taxes. Assuming the 1978 level of payroll taxes, this means that a person earning only $5,000 a year lost approximately 12.1 percent of wage earnings (6.05 percent levied on both the employer and the employee). However, the social security tax in 1978 was levied only on the first $17,700 of wages. Payroll taxes are not levied on wages in excess of the taxable wage base. As a result the total payroll tax burden on an individual earning $50,000 a year in 1978 was only 4.2 percent. The 1979 taxable wage base of $22,900 did not alter the regressive nature of the social security payroll tax appreciably.

The threat of an alarming outflow from the social security trust fund which gave rise to the recent increases in the payroll tax stems from the system's pay-as-you-go method of financing benefits. The tax revenues raised by current payroll taxes are not set aside to provide for future benefits but are essentially paid out as benefits to current retirees. The retirement benefits of current workers, in turn, depend upon tax revenues raised by taxing future generations of workers. Only a small amount of funds are kept in the trust fund to act as a safety reserve in case benefits temporarily exceed payroll tax receipts. The trust fund had assets of only $42 billion at the end of 1978, less than the total of one year's benefits.

The crisis in funding social security benefits began in 1972 when Congress passed legislation which increased benefits by 20 percent and tied future benefits to the cost of living. While it is quite reasonable to index benefits in order to protect the real value of a retiree's benefits from the effects of inflation, Congress made a serious mistake in specifying the benefit formula which ties future benefits to the cost of living. To illustrate the effects of the indexing formula, let us assume that prices rise by 10 percent. The increase in prices will increase the demand for labor,

---

[5]Milton Friedman, "Payroll Taxes, No; General Revenues, Yes," in Michael Boskin, ed., *The Crisis in Social Security: Problems and Prospects* (San Francisco: Institute for Contemporary Studies, 1977).

eventually building up the wage rate by 10 percent. Since the individual's future benefits are linked to one's earnings, they will automatically increase. But under the benefit formula legislated by Congress in 1972, all scheduled benefits would be increased by another 10%. This means that inflation would increase social security benefits by more than the cost of living and thus raise *real* benefits.

Soon after the 1972 hike in benefits, the rate of inflation surged to double-digit levels, and the economy entered its most serious recession since the 1930s. The combination of rising benefits and serious slump in the growth of revenues caused by unemployment seriously damaged the financial condition of the social security system. From 1970 to 1975, real benefits, after accounting for inflation, increased 56 percent while real GNP rose by only 10 percent. As a result, the Social Security Administration had to draw on the trust fund to finance current benefits. From 1976 to 1978, the outflows from the trust fund were more than $4.2 billion a year. At that rate, the trust fund would have been totally exhausted during the 1980s.

Even with the higher tax rates provided by the 1977 amendments, payments will overtake receipts in the mid-1990s, and the trust fund will again be in jeopardy.

In order to avert a crisis, Congress amended the Social Security Act in 1977 in several important respects. Social security payroll tax rates were to be increased in steps from the 6.05 percent rate in 1978 to 7.15 percent in 1986, and the taxable wage base from $17,700 in 1978 to $40,200 in 1986. In addition, the amendments modified the formula which indexes benefits to eliminate the unintended double adjustment for inflation. This combination of higher payroll tax revenue and lower benefits are expected to increase the assets of the trust fund to $84.8 billion by 1982.

Even though the 1977 amendments have temporarily averted a crisis in funding social security benefits, serious long-term problems still remain. The ability of the social security system to maintain the current ratio of benefits to previous earnings (in real terms) depends critically on the ratio of beneficiaries to contributing workers. During the early 1970s, the labor force grew very rapidly relative to the growth of beneficiaries because the children of the "baby boom" of the 1950s were entering the labor force. The total fertility rate (the average number of children born per woman) was above three from 1947 to 1964. This fertility rate declined sharply to 1.8 in 1978. This is even less than the 2.1 necessary to achieve zero population growth in the long run. This decline in the fertility rate will cause the growth of the labor force to decline sharply in the 1980s. If fertility rates remain at this low level, the social security system could have a serious problem in funding benefits when the postwar baby boom generation starts to retire during the years

2010 to 2030. Even if the fertility rate were to increase to 2.1, the number of beneficiaries for every 100 workers would rise from 30 in 1975 to 45 in 2030. This means that if the current ratio of benefits to previous earnings are to be maintained (in real terms), social security payroll tax rates would have to be increased by about 50 percent.

Unfortunately, the social security crisis will be with us for many years to come. The Social Security Amendments of 1977 did not solve the basic financial problems inherent in the program; they merely provided a temporary reprieve. Even with the higher tax rates provided by the 1977 amendments, payments will overtake receipts in the mid-1990s, and the trust fund will again be in jeopardy. Even more frightening is the long-run problem of financing the retirement of those born during the post-World War II baby boom. Faced with an incredible tax burden, it is extremely likely that the younger working age population will simply refuse to provide the current level of benefits to the elderly.

Alfred Kahn, President Carter's chief
inflation fighter, at a briefing March 23,
1979, called the price surge of 1.2 percent in
February a "bad performance" while again
voicing confidence that inflation will abate
this year. (United Press International
Photo)

13
Deregulating Transportation

On October 24, 1978, President Carter appointed Alfred Kahn as chairman of the Council on Wage and Price Stability. This appointment marked a subtle shift in the administration's anti-inflation program toward encouraging competition in the regulated sectors of the economy, particularly transportation. For some time, economists have pointed out that regulation does not always serve the best interests of consumers. In many instances, regulatory commissions have protected the industries they regulate from competitive pressures and have enabled the industry to act as a cartel to keep prices above competitive levels.

Alfred Kahn was an obvious choice to lead the fight for increased competition in the regulated sectors of the economy as he had taught regulatory and antitrust economics at Cornell University for 30 years. After serving as chairman of the New York State Public Service Commission for three years, he was appointed by President Carter to become chairman of the Civil Aeronautics Board (CAB) in 1977. It was as chairman of the CAB that Kahn first broke into public prominence as a strong advocate of free entry and competitive pricing. During his term, Kahn presided over a virtual deregulation of the airline industry.

Federal regulation of the airline industry started with the Air Mail Act of 1934. This piece of New Deal legislation curtailed competition in the airline industry by restricting entry into the industry and setting minimum airfares. This legislation, which made a cartel of the airline industry, was motivated by the serious financial difficulties faced by the infant airline industry during the Great Depression. In order to remain viable, the airlines required substantial government subsidies in the form of payments for airmail carriage. The act was designed to raise passenger fares so that airmail subsidies could be reduced.

The policy of restricting entry and keeping airfares above the competitive level continued with the creation of the CAB in 1938. Since then, not one new scheduled airline has received a "certificate of public convenience and necessity" which allows the airline to provide scheduled interstate service. The Civil Aeronautics Act of 1938 originally gave 16 airlines the right to operate on routes they were presently serving, but by 1974, the number had dropped to only 10 because of mergers.

In the late 1960s, the CAB became increasingly worried about excessive monopoly power of airlines in many city-pair markets. This concern prompted the CAB to liberalize their policy toward the entry of existing airlines into markets formerly served by only one carrier. By the 1970s, most principal markets were served by at least two airlines. However, the CAB still prevented competition on the basis of price. The CAB continued to maintain a regulated passenger airfares structure which was substantially above competitive levels. Since air carriers operating wholly within one state are not subject to CAB regulation, the tremendous difference between airfares in the unregulated California and Texas intrastate markets and the CAB regulated interstate markets provide striking evidence of the effect of CAB regulation on airfares. In the early 1970s, airfares in these intrastate markets were approximately 40 percent below the fares in similar interstate markets.

One might jump to the conclusion that higher airfares in the interstate markets enabled the regulated airlines to earn monopoly profits. This conclusion is not borne out by the evidence, however. Despite the higher fares, the CAB regulated airlines have had a very poor history of earnings since 1969, earning only about 5 percent on investment from 1969 to 1976. The poor earnings performance of the regulated airlines during the late 1960s and early 1970s coincide with the CAB's liberal policy toward the entry of additional carriers into formerly monopolized routes. When several airlines share the same market, nonprice competition tends to eliminate all excess profits. Since the CAB is prohibited by law from controlling scheduling, airlines compete primarily by adding flights in an attempt to increase their market shares. This nonprice competition led to a reduction in load factors causing the potential monopoly profits that would have resulted from the higher airfares to be eliminated by the increased costs per passenger of flying aircraft which are only 40 to 50 percent full. As a result, the higher airfares did not generate monopoly profits, they merely created excess capacity.

The movement to deregulate the airlines gained momentum during the Ford administration. In October 1975, President Ford submitted a proposal to Congress which would give airlines greater pricing flexibility and freedom to enter and exit specific markets. Similar proposals were introduced by Senator Howard Cannon of Nevada, Senator Edward Kennedy of Massachusetts, and Representative Glen Anderson of California. Despite bipartisan support for the policy of increasing competition in the airline industry, repeated attempts to pass legislation failed. The airline industry initially opposed deregulation because they feared that deregulation would have a negative impact on their earnings. They doubted that sufficient new traffic could be generated to offset the lower airfares. (As it turned out, however, the airlines seriously underestimated the amount of new traffic generated by the lower airfares.)

Moreover, many members of Congress feared that their district would lose its air service as a result of deregulation. The CAB requires airlines to serve many small communities at a loss. In essence, the CAB has to some degree promoted a policy of cross-subsidization, allowing carriers to make excess profits on some monopolized markets so that they can operate at a loss in other markets. Congressional members whose districts were favored by these cross-subsidies vigorously opposed any legislation which would allow greater freedom to enter and exit markets. Since the entry of new carriers to monopoly routes would eliminate the monopoly profits which were subsidizing unprofitable routes, the carriers would be forced to withdraw service to some small communities unless they were given direct subsidies to continue the service.

Despite vigorous congressional opposition to deregulation, the CAB under Chairman John Robson capitalized on a rare chance to demonstrate the benefits of price competition in the airline industry. In early 1977, the CAB approved a one-year trial of discount fares known as Super Saver Fares. These discount fares, which were originally proposed by American Airlines, reduced transcontinental airfares between New York and California by as much as 45 percent. When Alfred Kahn succeeded John Robson as chairman in April 1977, he continued the policy of encouraging discount fares. The Super Saver Fares between California and New York were followed by the Super Coach Fares which cut fares between Los Angeles and Chicago and the Florida No Frills Fares which reduced fares between Florida and the Northeast.

The growing availability of discount fares during Alfred Kahn's chairmanship at the CAB played an important role in producing the growth of traffic during late 1977 and 1978. The lower fares generated a large number of price-conscious passengers who would not have otherwise traveled. Domestic airlines carried about 20 percent more passengers in the first five months of 1978 than in the same period of 1977. Since the number of seats flown increased by only 7.2 percent during 1977, load factors increased from 54 to 62 percent. This increase in load factors more than offset the loss of revenue per passenger resulting from the discount fares. After earning only 5 percent on investment from 1969 to 1976, the rate of return turned around in the last half of 1977, and by 1978 the airlines were earning 11.6 percent on investment.

Of course, higher-load factors do reduce the quality of air travel somewhat. Excess capacity in the form of low-load factors does yield some benefits to the public. With higher-load factors, many flights sell out, reducing the probability of obtaining a seat on a preferred departure. And, of course, crowded flights are less comfortable. But the benefits of excess capacity are surely worth less than their cost.

The success of the discount fares greatly strengthened congressional support for deregulation of the airlines. Under the leadership of Senator Edward Kennedy, Congress finally passed legislation which would permit airlines to lower fares by as much as 50 percent and raise them by 5 percent without CAB approval. Moreover, the legislation provides for the automatic elimination of CAB regulation by 1982 unless it can be convincingly shown that it is worth retaining.

Since becoming chairman of the Council on Wage and Price Stability, Kahn has shifted his attention to encouraging competition in the trucking and railroad industries, which are regulated by the Interstate Commerce Commission (ICC). President Carter has made deregulation of both trucking and railroads one of the key elements in his "war on inflation." On June 22, 1979, he proposed legislation which would substantially reduce the ICC's control of truck freight rates, entry by truckers into new markets, and their expansion within markets. The legislation also calls for an end to all ICC truck regulation after 1982 unless the ICC can demonstrate a need for it.

Protection of the rate bureaus' monopoly power has kept freight rates in regulated trucking far above competitive levels and has made regulated trucking one of the most profitable industries in the United States.

The Interstate Commerce Commission was created in 1887 to regulate railway freight rates. During the 19th century, railroads exhibited a tendency toward "natural monopoly," a situation where average costs are greater than marginal costs. The rapid expansion of railway investment in track after the Civil War (a 325 percent increase in railroad right-of-way in only 22 years) created enormous fixed costs which had to be serviced out of current freight operations. These fixed costs of financing the investment in track and right of way were large relative to the marginal costs of carrying additional traffic. In order to cover these fixed costs, railroads had to charge some shippers freight rates that were substantially above the incremental cost of shipping the freight.

Prior to the creation of the ICC, the extent to which freight rates exceeded marginal costs depended primarily on the railroad's monopoly power over the shipper. Isolated shippers served by a single railroad were charged very high freight rates. On the other hand, markets which were served by two or more railroads were subject to frequent price wars which drove freight rates down to actual marginal cost. Because of competition from other railroads in the long-haul markets, railroads often charged higher fares for short hauls by isolated shippers than for long hauls. This practice of locational price discrimination caused considerable hostility among shippers in relatively isolated communities.

The Interstate Commerce Act of 1887 represented a political reaction against locational price discrimination. The legislation got its primary support from isolated western farmers and cattle owners who were especially exploited by the monopoly power of the railroads. However, many railroads also welcomed regulation because it prevented price competition in the long-haul markets where railroads were unsuccessful in avoiding costly price wars. The Interstate Commerce Act banned locational price discrimination and replaced it with a regulated fare structure which discriminated on the basis of "value of service."

Value-of-service pricing discriminates on the basis of the commodity being shipped. The highest fares are charged for shipping commodities whose demand is relatively insensitive to freight rates. Freight charges make up a very small portion of the price of high-valued manufactured goods; consequently, freight rates have a very small impact on demand. On the other hand, demand for bulk commodities such as coal is very sensitive to freight rates because transportation costs make up a large portion of their price. Under a value-of-service rate structure, most of the fixed costs of the railroad are borne by shippers of high-valued manufactured goods whose freight rates are substantially above marginal cost, while bulk commodities are carried at close to marginal cost.

The railroads did very well under ICC regulation until technological advances brought about considerable competition from trucking. Since railroad freight rates on high-valued commodities tended to be unduly high relative to the actual operating expense of carrying them, the truckers tended to concentrate on this type of traffic. In the face of trucking competition, the ICC's value-of-service fare structure was no longer viable. If freight rates for manufactured profits came down to meet competition from trucking, the burden of covering the fixed costs of track and right of ways would have to be shifted to agricultural and bulk commodities. Since demand for these commodities is very sensitive to changes in freight rates, the railroads feared that these markets would not be able to bear the increased fares to cover fixed costs. Faced with this dilemma, the railroads and the shippers of commodities favored by the cross-subsidization implicit in the ICC rate structure succeeded in getting Congress to pass the Motor Carrier Act of 1935 which extended rate regulation to interstate trucking firms.

Today about 40 percent of all intercity truck freight moves by truck carriers regulated by the ICC. These regulated carriers are required to obtain a "certificate of public convenience and necessity" from the ICC specifying the commodities they may carry and the routes on which they may operate. This regulated sector of the trucking industry has prospered under ICC regulation. In essence, the ICC has allowed these regulated carriers to act as a cartel in setting their rates. Representatives of the regulated firms meet regularly to set freight rates, and these "rate bureaus" are specifically exempt from the antitrust laws prohibiting price-fixing. Although individual carriers are permitted to file independent rates, these rates are subject to ICC approval. If the independent rates are lower than the cartel rate, the rate bureau can protest and the rate is usually suspended. This protection of the rate bureaus monopoly power has kept freight rates in regulated trucking far above competitive levels and has made regulated trucking one of the most profitable industries in the United States. The rate of return on equity for regulated trucking firms has averaged almost 20 percent in recent years.

The effect of regulation on freight rates is vividly illustrated by the decline in rates for certain products which were exempt from ICC regulation by the courts. During the 1950s a series of court decisions[1] held that poultry, frozen fruits, and vegetables were exempt from ICC regulation. After deregulation, freight rates for poultry declined about 33 percent and rates for frozen fruits and vegetables, 19 percent.

Of course, the regulated firms could not maintain their extraordinary profits without the ICC's policy of restricting entry into the regulated sector. Most of the "certificates of public convenience and necessity" existing today arose from the "grandfather clause" in the Motor Carrier Act of 1935 which granted certificates to those firms already in existence when the motor carrier industry originally came under federal regulation in 1935. Since that time, the ICC has been very reluctant to grant operating rights to new firms. In fact, the total number of trucking firms with operating rights has dropped from over 25,000 in 1939 to only 14,648 in 1974 through mergers and failures. New certificates are granted only when the applicant can demonstrate that its service will not damage the operations of any other carrier. Since any application is likely to produce many witnesses claiming hardship, few firms even bother to apply. Instead they usually buy certificates from existing carriers. Since the value of these certificates should be equal to the discounted value of the monopoly profits the certificate makes possible, they are very expensive. When Associated Transport went bankrupt in 1976, its operating rights, which were carried on its balance sheet at $976,000, were sold at public auction for over $20 million. The total market value of existing certificates may be as high as $3 to $4 billion.

The owners of the "certificates of public convenience and necessity" are not the only beneficiaries of the ICC's policy of cartelizing the regulated sector of the trucking industry. Regulation has also greatly strengthened the bargaining power of the International Brotherhood of Teamsters, who represent about 75 percent of the nonsupervisory employees in the regulated sector of the trucking industry. Because the ICC usually approves all rate hikes based on in-

---

[1]See Thomas Gale Moore, *Trucking Regulation Lessons from Europe* (Washington, D.C.: American Enterprise Institute, 1976).

creases in labor costs, management is under no pressure to bargain aggressively. The unionized trucking firms who dominate the rate bureaus know that the ICC will not only permit them to raise rates to cover any wage settlement but will also force these rates on nonunionized trucking firms. The ICC's policy of restricting entry into the industry also prevents new nonunion firms from entering the industry and competing for traffic carried by the unionized firms. As a result of this protection from nonunion competition, the Teamsters have been able to raise the wages of their drivers to a level about 50 percent higher than those in the unregulated sector.

Although about 60 percent of intercity truck freight is carried by unregulated trucking firms, these carriers are none the less affected by ICC regulation. The unregulated trucking firms consist of two categories: exempt carriers and private carriers. Exempt carriers transport unprocessed agricultural goods which were specifically exempt from federal regulation in the Motor Carrier Act of 1935. Private carriers are trucks owned by nontransportation businesses to deliver their own products to wholesalers or customers. Although these unregulated carriers are not required to obtain a "certificate" from the ICC, they cannot carry regulated commodities on a "for hire" basis. This restriction prevents the unregulated firms from operating in an efficient manner. An unregulated trucking firm can carry unprocessed agricultural products from rural areas to the cities, but it cannot carry nonagricultural products in the reverse direction. Similarly, a manufacturing company may haul its product to wholesalers, but it cannot haul goods back for another company even if that company is a subsidiary. These restrictions on the operations of the unregulated trucking firms results in excessive empty backhauling which inflates costs and wastes fuel.

As a result of protection from nonunion competition, the Teamsters have been able to raise the wages of their drivers to a level about 50 percent higher than those in the unregulated sector.

Although ICC regulation of trucking has succeeded in transferring income from consumers to the Teamsters and the trucking firms, it has failed to achieve its original objective of preventing the diversion of rail traffic to motor carriers. In fact, most studies indicate that ICC regulation has actually encouraged the diversion of traffic away from the railroads. The rate bureaus have used their power to raise rates primarily in the less-than-truckload sector of the industry, where railroads do not have a cost advantage. In the truckload sector of the industry, where the railroads can compete, the rates have been kept at competitive levels. Moreover, the ICC has tended to prevent the railroads from lowering their rates to effectively compete with the trucks in those markets. Recent studies indicate that in the absence of ICC regulation railway ton mileage could increase by as much as 20 to 36 percent by diverting traffic away from trucks.[2]

Tom Moore, an economist at Stanford University's Hoover Institute, has estimated the magnitudes of the effect on the regulated sector of the trucking industry using data from the year 1972.[3] He assumed that the regulated rates were approximately 20 percent higher than the competitive level. This means that shippers spent $3.4 billion more than if they had been able to ship at competitive rates. Of this $3.4 billion in excess freight charges, approximately $1.4 billion accrued to the owners of the certificates of convenience in the form of excess profits and about $1.7 billion accrued to Teamsters in the form of higher wages. The remaining $300 million is assumed to be wasted because the operating rights specify the routes the trucking firms must follow and thus increases the mileage they must drive.

The magnitude of these estimates shows why Alfred Kahn and the Carter administration have made deregulation of trucking a key element in their "war on inflation." Complete deregulation of the trucking industry would reduce freight rates in the regulated sector of the trucking industry by about 20 percent. Moreover, deregulation would permit the unregulated sector of the industry to carry a larger range of commodities and thus reduce empty backhaulage. Since this would reduce costs, unregulated trucking rates could decline by as much as 5 to 10 percent. This means that deregulation could reduce the overall price level by about .4 of a percentage point.

This reduction in the price level could be achieved, however, only if the deregulation is accompanied by a slight reduction in the money supply. Half of the reduction in the price level resulting from deregulation of trucking is due to the elimination of empty backhauling and circuity caused by regulatory restrictions. Therefore, the trucking industry should become more productive. With any given money supply, an increase in production will lower the price level. However, the other half of the reduction in the price level is due to the reduction in trucking profits and Teamster wages. Since the incomes of Teamsters and the owners of trucking firms will decline, so will their demand for money balances. This decline in the demand for money on the part of Teamsters and owners of trucking firms will cause an increase in prices elsewhere in the economy unless the money supply is reduced by a comparable amount. Thus, the .4 percentage point decline in the

[2]Thomas Gale Moore, "The Beneficiaries of Trucking Regulation," *Hoover Institute Occasional Papers* (Stanford University), Series 73-3.
[3]See R. W. Harbeson, "Toward Better Resource Allocation in Transport," *Journal of Law and Economics* (October, 1969); D. W. Woods and T. A. Domencich, "Competition between Rail and Truck in Intercity Freight Transportation," *Transportation Research Forum* (1971); and Stephen Sobotka and Thomas Domencich, "Traffic Diversion and Energy Use Implications: Another View," in *Regulation of Entry and Pricing in Truck Transportation,* ed. Paul W. MacAvoy and John W. Snow (Washington, D.C.: American Enterprise Institute, 1977).

price level resulting from deregulation implicitly assumes that deregulation of trucking is accompanied by a .2 percentage point decline in the money supply.

Although deregulation of trucking is supported by a wide range of both liberals and conservatives, it remains to be seen whether President Carter's proposal will succeed in becoming legislation. Deregulating trucking will be much more difficult than deregulating the airlines. The airlines were not earning monopoly profits as a result of regulation, and industry opposition was diluted by the fact that the airlines were split on the issue of deregulation. The regulated trucking industry and the International Brotherhood of Teamsters, on the other hand, have benefited greatly from ICC regulation. Moreover, the American Trucking Association and the Teamsters have been very generous contributors to political campaigns and have many powerful friends on Capitol Hill. It would be naive to assume that deregulating the trucking industry will be an easy task.

Paul Volcker, as he appeared before the Senate Banking, Housing, and Urban Affairs Committee in Washington on July 30, 1979, for consideration of his nomination as chairman of the Federal Reserve Board. (Wide World Photos)

14
Carter's Economic Policies: A Look Ahead

As we have seen, during the first two years of his administration, President Carter made rapid economic growth and a reduction in the unemployment rate key priorities in his economic policy. His Economic Report of the President issued in January 1978 confidently reiterated this emphasis on economic stimulation:

> In the period immediately ahead, growth in real output can proceed at a rate above its long-run trend without risking a resurgence of demand-induced inflation.[1]

As the year progressed, however, it became evident that this expansionary strategy was a serious mistake. Inflation turned out to be a far greater problem than had been expected. After rising at a 6.3 percent rate from the fourth quarter of 1976 to the first quarter of 1978, the rate of inflation (as measured by the GNP price deflator) accelerated to an 8.7 percent rate from the first quarter of 1978 to the first quarter of 1979. Most of this acceleration in the inflation rate can be directly attributed to Carter's stimulative policies during 1977 and 1978.

By late 1978, the political realities required Carter to shift his economic priorities. If the 9 percent rate of inflation could not be substantially reduced by the 1980 election, it would be almost a foregone conclusion that a Republican would be elected president. Finally realizing his predicament, Carter did an about-face on October 24, 1978 when he launched a new program of fiscal restraint designed to combat accelerating inflation. In a nationally televised speech, he promised to reduce the government deficit to less than $30 billion in fiscal 1980,

---

[1] *Economic Report of the President,* January 1978 (Washington, D.C.: Government Printing Office, 1978), p. 92.

almost $20 billion less than the deficit for fiscal 1978. As one step toward this goal, he imposed an immediate limitation on the hiring of federal employees to reduce the federal payroll by an estimated 20,000 employees during 1979.

More importantly, this movement toward fiscal restraint was accompanied by an extraordinarily restrictive monetary policy. After growing at an annual rate of over 9 percent from the fourth quarter of 1976 to the fourth quarter of 1978. The M_2 money supply slowed to an annual growth rate of only 2.7 percent in the period from October 1978 to March 1979. The M_1 money supply decelerated even more drastically. From a growth rate of over 8 percent from the fourth quarter of 1976 to the fourth quarter of 1978, the M_1 money supply actually fell at a 1.2 percent annual rate during the October to March period.

Monetary restraint is a necessary condition in order for any meaningful reduction in the rate of inflation to occur. Unfortunately, as a result of this restraint, a recession beginning in the second quarter of 1979 was almost inevitable. Output and employment bear the brunt of a restrictive monetary policy in the short run. The long-run benefits of a reduced rate of inflation become apparent only after people readjust their expectations to a reduced rate of monetary growth. Since it typically takes about two years for the full benefits of monetary restraint to become apparent, the rate of inflation can be expected to drop rather dramatically during the second half of 1980. Obviously the Carter administration has charted a very narrow course. The chances of Carter being reelected would be much greater if he had taken the anti-inflation stance of late 1978 about a year earlier. The stimulative economic policies of 1978 were simply bad economics and bad politics.

The length of the lag between a deceleration in the rate. of monetary growth and the resulting reduction in inflation depends critically upon how rapidly inflationary expectations adjust to conform to the new rate of monetary growth. It is obviously tempting for politicians to speed the adjustment of wage and price contracts to a reduced rate of monetary growth by imposing wage and price controls. Despite the fact that wage and price control programs always create shortages and distortions which reduce the efficiency of resource allocation in the long run, they are capable of breaking an inflationary psychology which keeps prices rising in the face of monetary restraint. President Nixon resorted to controls in 1971 for precisely this reason.

It is no surprise, then, that President Carter made wage and price guidelines the centerpiece of his anti-inflation program. Carter's wage and price guidelines had two key aspects. One was the 7 percent voluntary restraint on increases in wage and fringe benefits. The second was a voluntary limitation on prices which held specific price increases to rates one half of 1 percent lower than the average increases over the 1976–77 period. (Ironically, this implied that those who had raised prices the most in those years could do so again, while those who had contributed to price stability during those years would be punished by having lower permissible price increases.) Alternatively, if a company was unable to comply with the price deceleration rule because of uncontrollable increases in its costs, it could increase prices so long as profit margins were no higher than in the best two of the company's last three fiscal years.

In order to offer labor an incentive to comply with the voluntary wage guidelines, Carter included a "real wage insurance" provision which would have given tax rebates to workers complying with the 7 percent wage guideline if consumer prices rose more than 7 percent. For example, if the inflation rate were 9 percent, workers would receive a tax rebate equal to 2 percent of their wages. In order to place a ceiling on the costs of the provision, inflation rates above 10 percent would not have been covered, nor would wages and salaries in excess of $20,000. Thus the most that anyone could have received under the provision would have been $600. Even with this limitation, the cost of the program would have been considerable. The Carter administration estimated that the program would cost $2.5 billion if the inflation rate were 7.5 percent, and 47 million workers complied with the guidelines. By the time the proposal reached Congress in April, however, consumer prices had been rising at double-digit rates. At those inflation rates, the "real wage insurance" provision would have made Carter's goal of holding the 1980 deficit to less than $30 billion impossible. On April 4, 1979, the House Budget Committee effectively killed the proposal by eliminating it from the 1980 budget.

Without the "wage insurance proposal" to provide an incentive for compliance, the voluntary wage guidelines were unlikely to have much effect on the economy. Individuals rarely "voluntarily" act against their own self-interest. But the danger of the voluntary guidelines is that they may become mandatory at some future date. Fortunately, this is unlikely. Mandatory wage and price controls cannot be imposed without legislative authority which Carter does not currently possess.

In order for mandatory controls to be effective in holding down prices, they must be unanticipated. Nixon's wage-price freeze of 1971 had the advantage of surprise because the Economic Stabilization Act of 1970 gave him standby authority to control wages and prices. This sweeping grant of power to the president was contained in a brief amendment to a bill which extended the Defense Production Act of 1950 and set uniform accounting standards for the defense industry. The president was authorized to freeze prices, rents, wages, and salaries and to impose $5,000 fines for violations of the freeze. Without this standby authority, there probably would have been no controls. If it had been necessary for Nixon to ask Congress for the authority, the controls would have been much less effective.

President Carter has no such standby authority because Congress chose not to renew the Economic Stabilization Act of 1970 when it expired. Moreover, in passing the Council on Wage and Price Stability Act, Congress specifically stated that "This bill would grant no mandatory or standby control authority over the economy." In order for Carter to impose mandatory controls, Congress would have to debate and pass new legislation to authorize such controls. Any move in that direction would be counterproductive because it would generate widespread preemptive price increases, producing even more inflation.

Although Carter's guideline program is voluntary, it does have one enforcement weapon: the withholding of federal contracts from companies that violate the guidelines. The AFL-CIO and nine of its affiliated unions immediately challenged the legality of this enforcement weapon. Although U.S. District Court Judge Barrington Parker initially agreed with the AFL-CIO argument that the administration's procurement sanctions were an unconstitutional imposition of "mandatory" wage and price controls, the District of Columbia Circuit Court of Appeals reversed his ruling by a six to three vote. Chief Judge J. Skelly Wright, writing for the majority, said that the withholding of federal contracts was authorized by the 1949 Procurement Act. This act permits the executive to procure supplies in a manner "advantageous to the government in terms of economy, efficiency or service." While eliminating guideline violators from bidding on federal contracts might mean eliminating the lowest bidder, the court said it couldn't find a basis for rejecting the president's contention that withholding contracts from violators would save the government money and thus further "economy" and "efficiency." The Supreme Court's refusal to review the case, thus letting the D.C. Appeals Court ruling stand, was the first victory for the president's wage and price guideline program after a long series of defeats. However, by refusing to take the case, the U.S. Supreme Court left open the possibility that it could find the withholding of contracts illegal in some future case.

Carter's best course of action would be to admit . . . failure and abandon the attempt to use the procurement sanctions.

Although Carter may try to breathe life back into his guideline program by using the procurement sanctions against violators, this is a very crude and imperfect weapon to induce compliance. Some firms which are heavily dependent upon government purchases of their output can be influenced by the procurement policy. However, many firms do very little business with the government and thus are outside the range of government sanction. Moreover, the use of the procurement sanctions could place the government in the embarrassing position of worsening our balance of trade. For example, the Council on Wage and Price Stability has found the labor contract recently negotiated with the big rubber companies in "probable non-compliance." If the rubber companies fail to make their case, the government would have to buy tires from foreign companies or lose face on its threats to discipline violators.

Given the essentially voluntary nature of Carter's wage and price guideline program, there is very little chance that it will have much of an effect on wage or price decisions. Carter's best course of action would be to admit its failure and abandon the attempt to use the procurement sanctions. The failure of the guideline program is actually a blessing in disguise for the future well-being of the economy. Any short-run benefits derived from strict compliance with the guidelines would be outweighed by the long-run costs. Free market prices provide the signals which transfer resources to their most valuable use. If controls arbitrarily distort these price signals, resources flow into the wrong uses and productivity growth is reduced. Where prices are arbitrarily held down, production is discouraged and consumption is artificially subsidized. The resulting shortages produce the emergence of black markets or disguised price increases through uneconomical reductions in the quality of the product produced. If the Carter administration remains firm in its resolve to restrain the rate of total spending, the rate of inflation will eventually respond. The temptation to speed up this process of adjustment only leads to future inflationary pressures resulting from supply bottlenecks or a resurgence in inflationary expectations when the controls are removed.

Even without a guideline program, Carter's game plan was quite capable of satisfying his political needs. A mild recession in the second half of 1979 followed by a recovery in 1980 would create just the economic conditions necessary for his reelection. Unfortunately, just as the economy was entering the 1979–80 recession, the international oil cartel dealt this game plan a serious setback.

When Carter initially proposed his anti-inflation program in October 1978, a repeat of the 1973–74 oil crisis seemed impossible. Actually, the OPEC cartel had exhibited considerable weaknesses since 1974. The OPEC price increases during the last five years had been rather small; in fact, they had not even kept up with the rate of inflation. In real terms, the OPEC price of oil had actually fallen by about 20 percent since 1974. For most of 1978, there was a worldwide glut of oil that had induced many members of the OPEC cartel to give discounts in order to increase demand. Beginning in late 1978, the revolution in Iran, which led to the overthrow of the Shah, changed this oil glut into an acute shortage which enabled OPEC oil prices to surge again.

As a result of the upheaval, Iranian oil production virtually stopped for 69 days, causing a severe drop in world production. Iranian exports, which had been running at about 5.5 million barrels a day prior to the revolt, fell to zero late in December. Although other OPEC countries, principally Saudi Arabia, increased their production to partially offset the loss of Iran's exports, the net reduction in OPEC's exports was still about 2 million barrels a day. This is about the same reduction in world supply that occurred during the height of the Arab oil embargo in late 1973. When Iran resumed exporting oil on March 5, 1979, the new Khomeini government limited exports to 3 million barrels a day, approximately 55 percent of the volume exported during the Shah's reign. This presumably permanent loss of Iranian exports put OPEC in a position to boost the price of Arabian light crude oil (the benchmark price) from $12.70 in December to $18 in July, or a jump of 42 percent.

This second oil shock, coming almost exactly five years after the 1973 oil embargo, has focused renewed attention on the role that steadily rising U.S. oil imports have played in strengthening the OPEC cartel. American oil imports were only 3.5 million barrels a day in 1971 (about 25 percent of consumption). Since that time, they have risen to between 8.5 and 9 million barrels a day or over 45 percent of U.S. oil consumption. Without this rapid increase in U.S. imports which has expanded the market for their oil, the members of OPEC would have had great difficulty in maintaining their monopoly prices. For this reason, rising U.S. imports of OPEC oil have created serious political tensions between the United States and other industrial countries who are far more dependent than we are on imported oil. Moreover, as our imports have increased, our foreign policy has become increasingly subject to the influence of the oil exporting countries with sometimes damaging effects on our relationships with key friends and allies.

By simultaneously subsidizing consumption and discouraging domestic production, our energy policy has directly contributed to the rapid rise in the use of foreign oil.

One of the main reasons for this dramatic rise in our dependence on foreign oil is that all of the oil produced in the United States is subject to price controls. These price controls make a distinction between "old" and "new" oil. New oil refers to oil produced on a given property in excess of output in the same month of 1972. Its price is now set at $12.80 a barrel. The price of old oil is fixed at $5.80 a barrel. Because of these controls, the average price of domestic crude oil is only $9.50 a barrel, $8.50 less than the current OPEC benchmark price of $18. Since the price American consumers pay for oil is an average of the higher foreign crude oil price and the lower domestic price, the price controls subsidize the consumption of oil in the United States. At the same time, domestic production is discouraged by holding prices below the world level. By simultaneously subsidizing consumption and discouraging domestic production, the United States' energy policy has directly contributed to the rapid rise in the use of foreign oil.

Faced with the dramatic rise in OPEC oil prices and growing pressure from our allies to reduce our use of OPEC oil, President Carter was forced to change the disastrous energy policy we had pursued since 1973. The most important element of his new energy policy is the eventual decontrol of domestic oil prices. Under Carter's decontrol timetable, oil produced from wells on which drilling started after June 1, 1979 would be free of all price controls. Beginning on January 1, 1980, the prices of both old and new oil would be allowed to gradually rise to the world level so that all domestic crude oil would be free of controls by the end of 1981. To keep oil producers from reaping windfall profits, a tax would be imposed on the increased revenues resulting from the reclassification of old oil with the proceeds going to the Energy Security Corporation, a federally chartered corporation which will develop alternative sources of fuel.

President Carter also imposed quotas which would limit imports to an average of 8.2 million barrels a day in 1979 and to between 8.2 and 8.5 million barrels a day in 1980. However, these imports quotas are not expected to have much immediate effect. The Iranian revolution cut our imports so drastically during the first half of 1979 that we could import as much as 8.8 million barrels a day during the second half without exceeding the quota for 1979. Moreover, the fact that economic growth has seriously slowed down during the second half of 1979 makes it highly unlikely that we will exceed the 8.2 million barrels a day ceiling even without a quota system.

The decontrol of domestic oil prices is long overdue. Complete decontrol of domestic oil prices would directly reduce imports of foreign oil by as much as 1.3 million barrels a day by 1985. Unfortunately, the rise in the price of domestic oil will add to our inflation at a very inopportune time.

The combination of higher prices of OPEC oil and the decontrol of domestic oil prices will directly add about 3.5 percentage points to the GNP price deflator. However, under the program of gradual decontrol proposed by President Carter, this inflationary pressure will be spread out over the next three years. Since most domestic oil will remain at controlled prices during 1979, the direct impact of the rise in OPEC prices during the first half of 1979 will increase the general price level by only about 1.2 percentage points. However, as U.S. oil prices are allowed to rise to the world level during 1980 and 1981, Carter's decontrol plan will have the direct effect of raising prices by an additional 1.2 percentage points in each of those years as well. These estimates of the direct effect of higher oil prices on the price level assume that no further increases in the real price of oil will occur. They also neglect any feedback into wages. The increased price of OPEC oil has, of course, made us all poorer. If everyone decides that he or she must have the same real income as before, increased wage demands will fuel even more inflation.

The restrictive monetary policy pursued by the Federal Reserve from October 1978 to March 1979 virtually assured a recession starting sometime in the second quarter of 1979. Unfortunately, the higher prices for oil resulting from the OPEC increases and the decontrol of domestic oil will make that recession deeper than it otherwise would have been. If the Federal Reserve pursues the same monetary policy, the additional 1.2 percentage points of inflation during 1979 and 1980 will reduce real income by a similar amount. By the end of 1980, real output will be about 2.4 percentage points less and the unemployment rate .8 percentage points higher than they would otherwise have been.

Of course the length of the recession and the strength of the recovery depend critically upon Federal Reserve monetary policy during the second half of 1979 and the election year of 1980. After the extremely slow growth in the money supply from October 1978 to March 1979, the Federal Reserve resumed its expansionary growth in the money supply. From March to October 1979, the M_1 money supply increased at an annual rate of approximately 11 percent. The M_2 money supply increased at an even more rapid rate of about 12.5 percent. This rapid rate of monetary growth produced an apparent recovery from the recession during the third quarter of 1979. Unfortunately, it also produced renewed speculation against the dollar on foreign exchange markets. In response to the drop in the value of the dollar, Paul Volcker, Carter's newly appointed chairman of the Federal Reserve Board of Governors, announced on October 6, 1979, drastic new measures to reduce the growth of the money supply. At the time of this writing, it is too early to tell whether the Federal Reserve will persevere in slowing the rate of monetary growth. If it does, the recession will resume during the first quarter of 1980. This would cause political trouble for Carter in the primaries.

The major question is whether the Federal Reserve's anti-inflation program can survive the political pressures inherent in an election year. There is a real danger that Carter will not risk facing the electorate with an unemployment rate of 8 percent and will pressure the Federal Reserve into a return to an expansionary monetary policy. It is possible that he could postpone the inevitable acceleration of inflation until after the election, but such a strategy would ensure another dollar crisis and an even deeper recession in 1982. Under those circumstances, it is doubtful that history would treat him any kinder than it has Richard Nixon.

Index

—D—

vs. real wages, 46
Monopoly
  natural, 102
  of rate bureaus, 104
Moore, Tom, 106
Motor Carrier Act of 1935, 103, 104, 105
Mutual savings bank vulnerability to 30-year bonds, 33

—N—

National Bureau of Economic Research, 60, 85
National income
  relationship to GNP, 9
  relationship to stock of money held, 10
  relationship to total expenditures, 10
National Socialist Movement in Germany, 2
Natural monopoly, 102
New Deal, 99
New York State Public Service Commission, 99
Nixon, Richard, xviii, 46, 55, 57, 60, 61, 110, 111, 116
  surcharge on imports, 40
  wage and price controls, xii
Nominal income
  defined, 11
  relationship to money supply, 11, 12
Nordhaus, William, 24, 72

—O—

Official reserve transactions, 37
Oil
  dependence on foreign, 114
  embargo of 1973–1974, xviii, 66, 113, 114
Okun, Arthur, 45
Okun's Law, 45
Omaha (Nebraska) World Herald, 34
OPEC. See Organization of Petroleum Exporting Countries
Open Market Committee of the Federal Reserve System, 13, 14, 30
Open market operations, 14, 16, 31
  effects of on money supply, 15
Organization of Petroleum Exporting Countries (OPEC), xi, 67, 114, 115

—P—

"Paper profits," 6, 7
Parker, Barrington, 112
Pay Board, 56

Pay-as-you-go financing of social security, 93, 95
Peruvian anchovy catch, drop in 1972, 65
Phillips, A.W., 21
Phillips curve, 21, 22
  "accelerationist," xviii, 23
Political business cycle, xiii, 24, 25, 26, 72, 76
Politicians, short-run concern of, 23
Polls. See Public opinion polls
Population growth, rate of, 96
Post-war baby boom and social security, 96, 97
Presidential relationship to Federal Reserve, 25
Price Commission, 56
Price controls
  See also Wage and price controls
  on American oil, 114
  as cause of shortages, 56
Price-fixing, 104
Price index, 7
Price stability, relationship to unemployment, 21
Price supports, viii
Prices
  See also Cost
  relationship to expenditures, 19
  relationship to wages, 22
Printing of money. See Monetary expansion
Private carriers, 105
Procurement Act of 1949, 112
Procurement sanctions, 112
Production
  relationship to expenditures, 11
  relationship to GNP, 10
  relationship to income, 9
  relationship to monetary expansion, 20
Productivity
  effects of social security on, 93
  sources of increase in, 83
Profits
  "paper," 6, 7
  "windfall," 115
Property taxes, move to cut, 79
Proposition 13, vii, 79
Public opinion polls
  show acceptance of wage and price controls, xii
  show discontent, lack of confidence, vii
  show inflation as top priority, 75
Public sector imperialism, xii
Public-service job programs, effects of on employment, 54

—R—

Railroads
  deregulation of, 102
  regulation of, 103